CAMBRIDGE STREET LITERATURE

BOOKS BY PHILIP WARD

A Dictionary of Common Fallacies, 1978

Poetry

Collected Poems, 1960
Seldom Rains, 1967
At the Best of Times, 1968
The Poet and the Microscope, 1969
Maps on the Ceiling, 1970
A House on Fire, 1973
Impostors and their Imitators, 1977
The Keymakers, 1978

Drama

A Musical Breakfast, 1968
Garrity and other Plays, 1970
Pincers, 1973
Television Plays, 1976

Travel

Touring Libya, 3 vols., 1967-9
Tripoli, 1969
Touring Iran, 1970
Sabratha, 1970
Motoring to Nalut, 1970
Touring Cyprus, 1971
The Way to Wadi al-Khail, 1971
Touring Lebanon, 1971
Come with me to Ireland, 1972
The Aeolian Islands, 1973
Bangkok, 1974
Indonesia: a Traveller's Guide
(as 'Darby Greenfield'), 2 vols., 1975-6

Fiction and Essays

The Okefani 'Song of Nij Zitru', 1966
Ambigamus, or The Logic Box, 1967
Apuleius on Trial at Sabratha, 1968
The Quell-Finger Dialogues, 1969
A Lizard and other Distractions, 1969
A Maltese Boyhood, 1976

Librarianship

Simplified Cataloguing Rules (with R. Cave), 1959
A Survey of Libyan Bibliographical Resources, 1964
The Libyan Research Library Catalog, 1970
Planning a National Library Service, 1973
Indonesia: The Development of a National Library
Service, 3 vols., 1976

Literature

Spanish Literary Appreciation, 1969
Indonesian Traditional Poetry, 1975
The Oxford Companion to Spanish Literature, 1978

CAMBRIDGE STREET LITERATURE

Philip Ward

THE OLEANDER PRESS OF CAMBRIDGE

The Oleander Press
17 Stansgate Avenue
Cambridge CB2 2QZ

ISBN 0 900891 21 1 soft cover
ISBN 0 900891 52 1 hard cover

British Library Cataloguing in Publication Data

Ward, Philip
Cambridge street literature. – (Cambridge town, gown and county: vol. 22).
1. Cambridge – History – Sources
I. Title II. Series
942.6'59'008 DA690.C2

Front cover illustration: An Almanacke, for the yeere of our Lord God 1646.

Back cover illustration: The Street-Stationer. *c*.1849

Title-page illustration: A Long-Song Seller, *c*.1849

Designed by Ron Jones

Printed and bound by The Burlington Press, Foxton

Introduction

By 'street literature', the compiler of this illustrated survey understands almanacks; broadsheets; ballads, cocks and catchpennies; chapbooks; posters intended for display on public buildings and walls, and handbills for distribution to advertize plays, sporting events, and wares of any kind. By 'Cambridge' is understood either the theme of the publication, or the place of printing or publication. Street literature printed outside Cambridge has been sold and distributed there, while matter printed in Cambridge has frequently been distributed outside the city and county.

The present survey excludes, for no better reason than limitation of space, such literature as books and pamphlets; newspapers and periodicals; the Bible and its distribution; the rise of popular fiction, comic strips, penny readings, and series of cheap classics; and such complex questions as the evolution of the Cambridge book trade, and the question of literacy in its context of schools, libraries, and adult education.

The mass of ordinary people in England have never had enough education for the appreciation of full-length books, or sufficient leisure to read them if they had the learning. In the middle of the 18th century the cheapest book cost 2s 6d for an octavo, while a quarto might well cost 10s and a folio as much as 13s and more. In Cambridgeshire and the countryside generally, the price of a book might well represent a week's wages, and chapbooks represented real continuity with (however garbled) accounts of past events and such lore as children's games and nursery rhymes. Until the spread of newspapers in the 1850s and the gradual implementation of compulsory education from the 1870s, almanacks, penny broadsheets and chapbooks formed the sole reading-matter to be found in many poorer homes, and no study of literature in England is complete without a respectful reference to the broadside ballad or chapbook, those ambassadors of literacy.

Almanacks

"Looke in the Almanac, finde out the Moone-shine", cried bully Bottom, and readers have never ceased to do so.

An almanac[k] is a single sheet or book consisting of a calendar of a given year, together with a series of astronomical or astrological observations, and a register of ecclesiastical festivals together with, in the majority of cases, a list of secular feasts and fairs connected with trade. As *fasti*, the almanacks were known to the Romans, though our word is derived from the Arabic *al-manakh*, rendered as 'calendar' in an Arabic-Spanish dictionary of 1505, and it is most likely that the type of almanacks still sold is of oriental origin. Such was the popularity of the almanack, that it benefited almost instantaneously from the invention of printing: the first printed almanack known (that of Pürbach) dates from before 1461. In England the first almanack recorded is *The Kalendar of Shepardes*, a translation from the French printed by Richard Pynson about 1497.

In the 16th century, almanacks began to offer predictions or 'prognostications', and were consequently frequently known by the latter name. Such early 'prognostications' included Leonard Digges' *Prognostication Everlasting of Right Good Effect* for 1553 and later years; and John Partridge's *Mercurius Redivivus* for 1681. Pope immortalized Partridge's name in *The Rape of the Lock,* while Swift went so far as to burlesque Partridge's style and to predict his death in the true prognosticator's manner.

One of the most celebrated compilers of almanacks was the Cambridge graduate Dr Bomelius, who later went to Russia, where he lived in pomp as royal physician at the Court of Ivan. Bomelius, who was alleged to have urged the Tsar to marry Elizabeth I, turns up again as a tenor rôle in Rimsky-Korsakov's opera *The Tsar's Bride*, set in 1572 and first performed in 1899. It is worth recalling in this context that calendars and almanacks were always the most international of early books, for even those countries which kept mutually conflicting calendars could 'benefit' from the long-term prognostications, which were of course only remembered the year after if they were proved correct.

Carroll Camden, Jr., differentiated prognostications from almanacks by a dubious division of their audience: prognostications, he claimed, were intended for popular use, whereas almanacks were originally intended for students of law and physicians. When the serious study of astronomy began, about 1540, the prognostications and almanacks were bound up with calendars and sold for about 1d each. A dubious division, for, at least as late as 1635, the Cambridge almanack *Speculum mundi* by John Swan asserted:

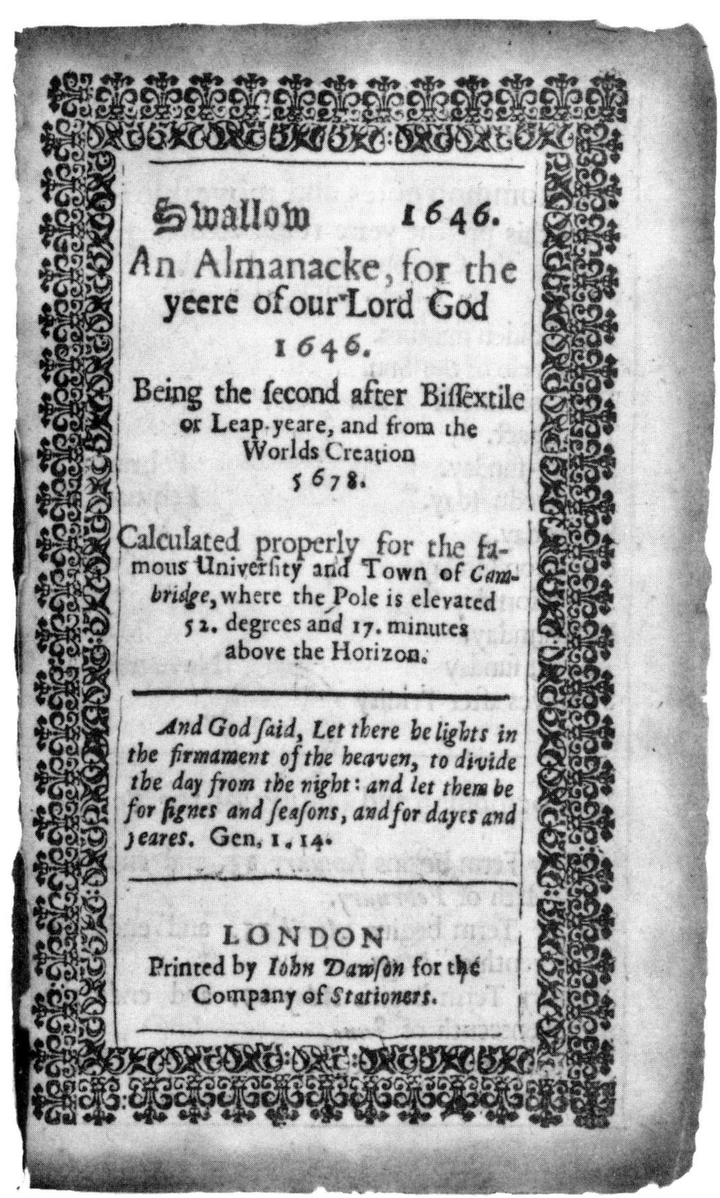

Swallow 1646.

An Almanacke, for the yeere of our Lord God 1646.

Being the ſecond after Biſſextile or Leap-yeare, and from the Worlds Creation 5678.

Calculated properly for the famous Univerſity and Town of *Cambridge*, where the Pole is elevated 52. degrees and 17. minutes above the Horizon.

And God ſaid, Let there be lights in the firmament of the heaven, to divide the day from the night: and let them be for ſignes and ſeaſons, and for dayes and yeares. Gen. 1. 14.

LONDON
Printed by *Iohn Dawſon* for the Company of *Stationers*.

An Almanacke, for the yeere of our Lord God 1646 . . . Swallow. Book almanack 'calculated properly for the famous University and Town of Cambridge' and printed in London by John Dawson in [1645]. 15 x 9½ cm. (*Cambridge University Library*)

'Eclipses, coniunctions, prodigious sights, flashings, comets, new starres, what are they but Oracles of God?'. Astronomy was indeed a dog with the tin-can of theology tied to its tail long after that.

The Swallow almanack for 1646 illustrated here is characteristic of the genre. On the verso of the cover/title-page is a list of the movable feasts; p.3 (A2) is 'A Computation of the Six Ages of, the world'; p.4, 'The natures of the 7. Planets'; pp.5-16, a page for each calendar month, including a long-range weather forecast.

A new 24-page section begins with a new title-page: *The latter part of this Almanack for the yeare Of our Lord God*. Printed by Bern. Alsop, for the Co. of STATIONERS. This imprint shows that the same or several different almanacks could share the same perpetual data, appended to a changing calendar. That they not only could, but did, is proved by the title-page verso, corresponding to p.18, beginning "The Characters of the Planets, &c.', which duplicates in concept p.4 of the opening 16-page section. The rest of the perpetual section consists of: pp.19-20, 'The day and houre of the Sunnes entrance into the foure Cardinall signs'; pp.21-22, continuation of the foregoing and 'Of the Eclipses and A Chronologicall note of some memorable Accidents, shewing how long it is since any of them happened' [two 'Accidents' being the destruction of Jerusalem by Titus, dated to 1576 years previous; and Cambridge being made a University, dated somewhat optimistically to 1011 years previous]; p.23, 'Of the four Cardinall winds . . .'; pp.24-25, 'Of Blood-letting and some other Physical Observations'; pp.26-29, 'Other Notes fit to be knowne', including 'Observations concerning the Weather' on p.27, and 'Observations for Husband-men and others' on pp.28-29; p.30, 'A Table of the Kings of England'; p.31, 'A Table shewing the houre and minute of the suns setting every second day in the yeare'; pp.32-38, 'The principall Faires of England and Wales'; and pp.39-40, 'A Note of the moveable Faires in England'.

It is perhaps startling at first sight that more almanacks were printed in Cambridge than in any other English provincial city, for its population could certainly not have sustained sales of such a magnitude. One of the reasons for the pre-eminence of Cambridge (and, to a lesser extent, of Oxford), can be traced to an infringement of the monopoly of almanack-printing enjoyed by Londoners during the reign of Elizabeth I, ratified by a patent granted by James I in 1603 to the Stationers' Company. Cambridge University Press was admonished for infringing this patent; then the Privy Council decreed on 29 November 1628 that the University Press was permitted only those almanacks of which the first copy was brought to them. Further orders of the Privy Council were made on 10 December 1623 (substituting the word 'Prognostication' for 'Almanack') and on 23 January 1625 (pronouncing 'Prognostication' to denote the same as 'Almanack'). Yet the Company was still complaining, in 1624, in a memorial to the Privy Council, that Cantrell Legge had printed Pond's Almanack, of which the Company possessed sole copyright.* How the

* E.F. Bosanquet, 'English *17th century almanacks'* (London, 1930).

matter was resolved is not clear, but the University Press continued to print one version of Pond's Almanack for the rest of the century, and the Stationers' Company another.

It was only as late as 1775, indeed, that the Court of Common Pleas decided that the virtual monopoly of almanack-printing could not be upheld, thus opening the way for the flood of badly-printed and fraudulent almanacks based chiefly not on their calendar but on their predictions. Cambridge University Press was given, in compensation for the loss of their share of the monopoly, a Treasury grant of £500 a year, still paid and still the Press's sole subsidy from an outside source, according to the former Printer, Brooke Crutchley.

Another reason for the importance of Cambridge as a centre for almanack-printing is that there were sufficient capacity, continuity, and trained printers in Cambridge to guarantee the prompt appearance of ephemera which depended for their rapid and widespread sale on the regularity of their appearance. Thus, one does not have to postulate a huge market for almanacks in Cambridge to explain the large number of titles, and correspondingly high output of copies, disseminated not only across London but also throughout the rest of England.

The price of almanacks in 1611 was about 2d for 20 or 24 leaves. This price gradually rose to '9d stiched' in the middle of the 18th century; and to 16d (including 4d duty) in 1798.

Between 1600 and 1640 alone, some 69 writers of almanacks are listed in Pollard & Redgrave's *Short-title catalogue of books printed in England . . ., 1475-1640* (London, 1926; reprinted 1946). The earliest Cambridge almanack with a location in *STC* is no. 405, printed by Cantrell Legge in 1625. H.R. Plomer, writing in 1885, had already identified 160 different almanacks published during the 17th century; subsequently several dozen more have been noted.

Locations recorded in Pollard & Redgrave, and in Wing's *Short-title catalogue of books printed in England . . ., 1641-1700* (New York, 1945), indicate that the libraries richest in Cambridge almanacks are the British Library; the Bodleian Library, Oxford; Cambridge University Library; and to a much lesser extent Harvard, Yale, the Folger Library, and Trinity College, Dublin. Only a very few early almanacks are in the Cambridgeshire Collection in Cambridge Central Public Library, Lion Yard, off Petty Cury. The first is Swallow for 1642, followed by the *Cambridge Memorandum-book for the year 1764* and . . . *1769*; the Norfolk, Suffolk, Essex & Cambridgeshire almanac for the year 1786; and the *Cambridge Express* almanac 1907 and 1908.

These are the holdings of Cambridge almanacks from 1626 to 1707 in the Bodleian Library, which has absorbed the great collections of Ashmole, Douce, Rawlinson and Wood:

Year	*Almanack*
1626	Pond
1629	Clarke; Rivers
1630	Pond; Rivers
1631	Butter; Kidman; Pond
1632	Pond
1633	Pond
1634	Kidman; Pond; Winter
1635	Kidman
1636	Booker; Dove
1638	Rivers; Swallow; Winter
1639	Swallow
1641	Dove; Pond
1649	Pond
1651	Pond; Swallow
1652-5	Dove; Pond; Swallow
1656	Dove; Pond
1657-9	Dove; Pond; Swallow; Swan
1660	Dove; M.F.; Pond; Swallow
1661	Dove; M.F.; Swallow; Swan
1662	Dove; Pond; Swallow; Swan
1663	Dove; M.F., Pond; Swan
1664-5	Dove; M.F.; Pond; Swallow; Swan
1666-7	Dove; Pond; Swallow; Swan
1668	Clarke; Dove; Hooker; Pond; Swallow; Swan
1669	Dove; Pond; *Protestant Almanack*; Swallow; Swan; Whiting
1670	Dove; Pond; Swallow; Swan
1671	Dove; Fly; Pond; Swallow; Swan
1672-3	Dove; Pond; Swallow; Swan
1674-5	Dove; Fly; Pond; Swallow; Swan
1676-9	Dove; Pond; Swallow; Swan
1680-1	Culpepper; Dove; Fly; Pond; Swallow; Swan
1682	Culpepper; Dove; Fly; Swallow; Swan
1683-4	Culpepper; Dove; Fly; Pond; Swallow; Swan
1685	Culpepper; Dove; Pond; Swallow
1686-7	Culpepper; Dove; Fly; Pond; Swallow
1689	Dove; Pond
1690	Culpepper; Dove; Pond; Swallow
1691	Fly; Pond; Swallow
1692	Culpepper; Dove; Fly; Pond; Swallow
1693	Dove; Pond
1694	Culpepper; Dove; M.F.; Fly; Pond; Swallow
1695	Culpepper; Dove; Fly; Pond; Swallow
1696	Culpepper; Dove; Fly; Pond
1697	Dove; Fly; Pond
1698-1703	Culpepper; Dove; Fly; Pond; Swallow
1704-6	Dove; Pond
1707	Dove

Table 1

Total Number of Almanacks Printed in Cambridge in the 1660s

Almanack	*1664*	*(unsold)*	*1665*	*(unsold)*	*1666*	*(unsold)*	*1667*	*(unsold)*	*1668*	*(unsold)*
Pond's	24,800	(2,100)	24,900	(4,075)	22,850	(5,000)	19,750	(14,725)	14,000	(400)
Dove's	24,850	(2,900)	24,900	(3,900)	22,825		22,500		14,250	
Swallow's	24,850	(–)	24,900	(–)	24,900	(3,500)	24,850	(7,325)	18,500	(50)
Swan's	7,900	(500)	8,000	(–)	7,950	(300)	7,850	(1,150)	4,700	(–)
Clarke	–		–		–		–		4,400	(100)
	82,400	(5,500)	82,700	(7,975)	78,525	(8,800)	74,950	(23,200)	44,850	(550)

(Adapted from C. Blagden, *Distribution of almanacks in the second half of the seventeenth century*, in *Papers of the Bibliographical Society of the University of Virginia*, vol.11, 1958).

The large numbers of competing almanacks printed in Cambridge had reached their peak of popularity by the mid-1660s, the demand falling by about 4,000 a year until 1667, when a drop of some 20,000 occurred. This led as one might expect to a drop of 20,000 in the printings ordered in 1668, and in effect this was a shrewd judgment, as the sharp fall in unsold stock for that year proves. Yet the heyday of the almanack was over, as the following figures for Cambridge printings of leading almanacks in the 1880s will show:

Table 2

Total Number of Almanacks Printed in Cambridge in the 1680s

Almanack	*1685*	*1686*	*1687*
Pond's	8,000	6,000	7,150
Dove's	11,000	9,000	7,000
Swallow's	16,000	16,000	16,350

[Swan's had ceased publication in 1684]

N.B. The odd quantities in the table of printings of leading almanacks in the 1660s and 1680s are due to the retention in Cambridge of a certain number for local sale.

The Bowes Catalogue of Cambridge books (Cambridge 1894) contains almanacks for 1626 (for the meridian of Cambridge, by W. Strof); for 1627 (Dove, Crost, Lakes, Rivers, Strof and Waters); 1629; 1634 (Clark, Dove, Kidman, Rivers, Swallow, Turner, Winter); 1635 (the broadsheet Almanack for 1636); 1640 (Rivers, Swallow); and the intriguing *Olympia Domata, or an almanack for the year of our Lord God 1689 . . . for the Town of Stamford* . . . by John Wing. Printed by John Hayes, Printer to the University, Cambridge. 1689.

As well as almanacks in book form, almanacks in single sheets were produced, for hanging on walls. Due to their large format and to the small point-size of types used, these sheet almanacks were capable of exhibiting almost as much information as a conventionally bound almanack.

Known holdings of the broadside *Cambridge Almanack* by M.F. in Cambridge University Library are: 1636, 1664, 1668, 1670-83 (all printed in Cambridge; one illustrated here), 1710 ('printed for the Company of Stationers at London by J. Heptinstall') and 1774-1834. The title changes in 1816 to the *Norfolk, Suffolk, Cambridgeshire, Isle of Ely, Huntingdonshire and Bedfordshire Almanack for the year of our Lord 1816*. As a guide to prices, the almanacks for 1774-6 cost 6d (2½p) each; 1777-9, 5d; 1780, 6d; 1781, 5d; 1782-91, 7d; 1792-7, 8d; 1798-1801, 13d; 1802-4, 14d; 1805-15, 1/7d (*c*. 8p); 1816-34, 2/0, except 1817, 6d.

The sheet almanacks are nearly all a uniform 56 cm high x 44 cm wide. The calendar is supplemented by a steadily-changing range of information: compare the data on the 1675 almanack illustrated with the data provided under the heading 'Cambridgeshire' in the 1894 *Norfolk . . . Almanack*: names of the Lord Lieutenant, the Custos Rotulorum of the Isle of Ely and Bishop of Ely; the Members of Parliament; officials of the University of Cambridge and professors; fairs and quarter sessions; and county council, county courts, and bankers.

Among the sheet almanacks in the Bodleian Library, Oxford, are issues of

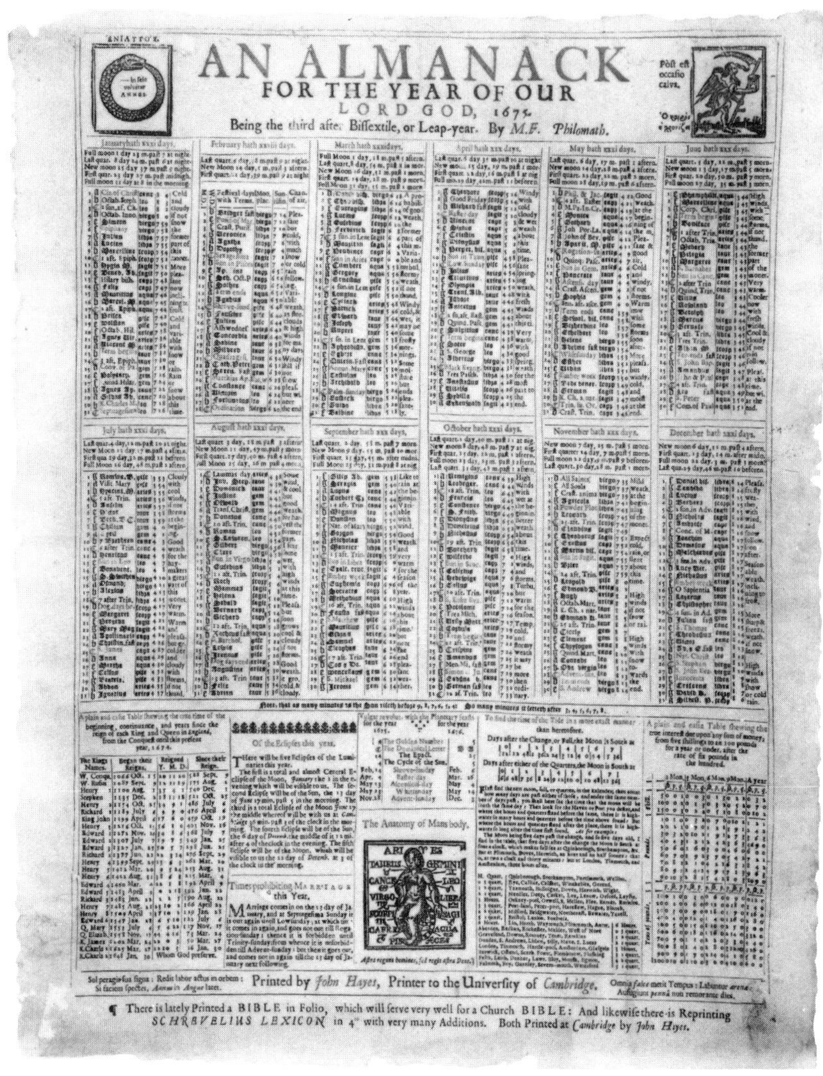
AN ALMANACK FOR THE YEAR OF OUR LORD GOD, 1675.

Being the third after Bissextile, or Leap-year. By *M.F. Philomath.*

Printed by *John Hayes*, Printer to the University of *Cambridge*.

There is lately Printed a BIBLE in Folio, which will serve very well for a Church BIBLE: And likewise there is Reprinting *SCHREVELIUS LEXICON* in 4° with very many Additions. Both Printed at *Cambridge* by *John Hayes*.

An Almanack for the Year of our Lord God, 1675 . . . By M.F. Sheet almanack printed by the University Printer, John Hayes [1674]. 56 x 44cm. (*Cambridge University Library*)

The Cambridge Almanack by M.F. for the year 1740, 'Printed at London by T. Wood for the Company of Stationers', and the same compiler's almanacks (all printed by W. Burton) for 1724, 1726, 1728, and 1729. Bodley's John Johnson Collection also contains *A Perpetual and Universal Table readily shewing the day of the month and of the week by Edmund Carter, writing master in Cambridge,* with the imprint 'Cambridge. Printed for the Author. MDCCXLIII'.

The Cambridge Almanack was founded in 1857 by the bookseller and printer F.W. Talbot, 19 Sussex St. It was issued annually until 1881, when its title changed to *The Cambridge Almanack and Diary*, reverting to the original title from 1882 to 1898, when it is believed to have ceased. The Cambridgeshire Collection holds the volumes for 1872-98 only. The usual contents can be judged from the cover-title of the 1872 issue, of 44 pages (including covers): *The Cambridge Almanack for 1872, containing a useful and entertaining calendar, Cambridge postal arrangements, including the times of closing the various pillar letter boxes and receiving houses; a list of the aldermen and councillors, justices of the peace, and corporate officers of the Borough; the Cambridge and Chesterton Boards of Guardians; Committees of the Council & Guardians; Parish Commissioners; omnibus and cab fares; a list of the churches and chapels in Cambridge, with the hours of service. 19 illustrations, with descriptive notes. Stamps, taxes, university and law terms, rates of postage, eclipses, and much other useful and interesting matter.* The price of the 1872 almanack was 2d (less than 1p), while the taxi fare then from the centre to the railway station or vice versa was 1s 0d (5p).

Another popular almanack distributed in Cambridge was *A. Sidney Campkin's Illustrated Cambridge Almanack* established in 1875 as an advertising medium for Campkin's of 11 Rose Crescent. Campkin was a dispensing and manufacturing chemist. His 15th issue for 1889 bound 20 pages of his own advertisements around a standard national almanack of 32 pages which consisted of the usual calendar pages and excellent copper engravings of Orgueil Castle in Jersey and the Vale of Avoca, among others; proverbs; and characteristic Victorian verses on love and death. Campkin advertises many of his wares, such as Pryor's Noted Tea Dust and The Cambridge Hair Regenerator. Campkin's almanacks were issued free to customers, much as calendars or diaries are given to important clients today. As an indicator of the rising cost of postage which we seem to take (needlessly?) for granted nowadays, it is interesting to note that the postal rate for weights of 1 oz. and below in 1888 was 1d, while in 1914 the same cost was valid for weights of 4 oz. and below. By 1925, the rate had increased to 1½d. The 40th issue of Campkin's almanack advertised Tomlinson & Co.'s Butter Powder, and included extracts from *The Christian World* for 27 November 1913 on 'Friendly Societies and the Insurance Act' and from *The Daily Chronicle* of the same month on 'The American Woman as she really is', features which offer an interesting view of the almanack as a magazine of the digest type. Holdings of Campkin in the Cambridgeshire Collection are: 1889, 1890, 1911-15, 1925, 1931, 1936, 1937, and 1940, the last being apparently the final volume to appear.

The British Library (where they are entered under 'Ephemerides') possesses other 19th-century almanacks published in Cambridge. *The Cambridge University Almanack* for 1801 (published like most almanacks in the preceding year to be ready for use on 1 January of the appropriate year), for 1802-9, 1812-13, 1816, 1833, etc. *The Cambridge University General Almanack and Register* volumes for 1843-58 are held in the British Library, which also possesses *The Cambridge Year-Book and University Almanack* for 1862, ed. by W. White, published in Cambridge in 1862.

The all-pervading influence of the almanack, despite its absurd predictions and its dishonest claims to past success while ignoring all failures, can be measured by the fact that the *Foulsham's Original Old Moore's Almanack 1978* that I picked up from my local newsagent in Cambridge before Christmas 1977 (64 pp. for 12p), claims a certified net sale averaging 1 million copies. Features additional to the basic calendar include 'Greyhound Racing Numbers Forecasts', a talisman showing the Sun for £1, a crystal ball and booklet for £4.50, and an astrological study of TV-personality Bruce Forsyth which on no occasion succeeds in spelling his name correctly.

Further Reading

Blagden, Cyprian. 'The distribution of almanacks in the second half of the seventeenth century'. In *Papers of the Bibliographical Society of the University of Virginia*, Vol. 11, 1958.

Bollème, Geneviève. *Les almanachs populaires aux XVIIe et XVIIIe siècles*. Paris, 1969. [Essential comparative material, given the paucity of English-language studies of the popular almanack].

Bosanquet, Eustace F. *English printed almanacks and prognostications: a bibliographical history to the year 1600*. London, 1917.

Bosanquet, Eustace F. 'English 17th century almanacks'. In *The Library*, 4th ser., vol. X, 1930.

Camden, Carroll, *Jr*. 'Elizabethan almanacks and prognostications'. In *The Library*, 4th ser., vol. XII, 1931.

Heywood, A., *Jr*. *Three papers on English almanacs*. Manchester, 1904.

Ballads and Broadsides

Clown	What hast here? ballads?
Mopsa	'Pray now, buy some: I love a ballad in print o' life, for then we are sure they are true.
Autolycus	Here's one to a very doleful tune, how a usurer's wife was brought to bed of twenty moneybags at a burden; and how she longed to eat adders' heads, and toads carbonadoed.
Mopsa	Is it true, think you?
Autolycus	Very true; and but a month old.

Shakespeare, *The Winter's Tale*, IV, iii.

The terms 'broadside' and 'broadsheet' are often used interchangeably but, in generally-accepted parlance, a broadsheet can be defined as a sheet printed on both sides but not folded (as a chapbook is folded), whereas a broadside is printed on one side only, usually in two columns. A half-sheet is roughly 51 x 76 cm and a quarter-sheet approximately 51 x 38 cm. The usual text found on broadsides is the ballad, a traditional narrative song originally intended to be sung as an accompaniment to dancing, but later applied indiscriminately to any type of narrative rhyme printed on broadsides.

Since the term 'broadside ballad' is so widespread, it is becoming less usual to consider prose sheets as broadsides. One frequently comes across the terms 'cocks' and 'catchpennies' in the field of street literature. 'Cocks' are broadsides printing spurious news which could be revived at any place ('a widow of THIS NEIGHBOURHOOD!') or at any time ('seduction of YOUNG LADY YESTERDAY!') in the absence of broadsides describing real events. Catchpennies are deceptive and usually hasty broadsides produced to earn a quick profit by fraud from a non-existent twist to sensational but legitimate news.

A ballad slip, or slip ballad, also known as a single slip, is a single-column ballad sheet usually cut from a double-column ballad sheet and sold, at half the price of the double sheet, for a halfpenny (½d), in districts where the chaunters or patterers found that they could not sell ballads at a penny (1d).

Ballads have always been an integral part of oral tradition and, though they have changed, there are some remarkable instances of unmarred continuity.

Cecil Sharp recounts, for instance, in his *English folk song: some conclusions* (4th ed., 1965), that the eleven verses of 'Robin Hood and the Tanner' sung by the blind Somerset singer Henry Larcombe corresponded almost word for word with the same verses on a blackletter broadside in the Bodleian Library collected by Anthony Wood, who died in 1695.

Even conceding that broadsides are defective in their poetry, they should not be neglected by the careful literary historian, any more than stinging nettles should be neglected by the systematic botanist.

A sequence of Robin Hood ballads was published by Wynken de Worde in or about 1495, according to William Chappell (or some ten years later, according to other authorities).

In actual practice, the English *broadside* ballad did not of course exist before the introduction of printing, but it is not accurate to assert, as Gummere does, that 'street ballads begin about 1540', or even to call Thomas Skelton's ballad on Flodden Field (1513) the beginning of the genre, for it is merely the earliest extant English printed ballad. No: this is a question to which the answer has been lost.

We simply have no idea when ballads were first written down, much less when they were composed for oral dissemination. Hyder E. Rollins identified at least seventy printers of ballads at work before the tenth year of Elizabeth I's reign. If one recalls that Rollins uses the term 'printer' to subsume 'stationer' (that is, printer or bookseller or both), then one could easily arrive at a figure of 150 printers by taking into account the whole of the period to 1600.

Beginning in the mid-16th century, broadside printers were required to register their ballads with the Stationers' Company in London and, though clearly not all of them did so, the registers of the Company provide a representative list of some three thousand popular street ballads between 1557 and 1709. These ballads were mostly in 'blackletter' (the Gothic-style typeface), with crude woodcuts used both appropriately and, often, also hilariously inappropriately. They were collected by those with sufficient means, pasted on walls and doors, and exchanged by youths of all classes with the zeal shown by later generations in swapping comics and stamps. Samuel Pepys, that celebrated Cambridge collector, bought the important ballad collection of the antiquary John Selden, and added many more.

The ballad collection in the Pepysian Library of Magdalene College consists of more than 1700 broadsheet ballads pasted into five large albums; 964 are said to be unique surviving copies. Hyder E. Rollins has edited and published many of these ballads in his *A Pepysian garland: black-letter broadside ballads of the years 1595-1639. Chiefly from the collection of Samuel Pepys* (Cambridge, Mass., 1922) and the eight volumes collectively known as *The Pepys ballads (1553-1702)* (Cambridge, Mass., 1929-32).

There are few positive references to the sale of ballads in Cambridge, and even W. Carew Hazlitt is mistaken when he asserts in his elaborate edition of Thomas Warton's *History of English poetry* (vol. 4, p.109) that "a very curious MS. at Oxford . . . shows that in 1520 the ballad, the *Not-browne*

Mayde, was on sale at the sister University in the form of a broadside, price one penny". The stall in question was in Oxford, not in Cambridge, but the sale of ballads may have been no less notable in Cambridge.

The earliest extant broadside ballads printed at Northampton by Raikes and Dicey, and thus made available through their distribution network in Cambridge in the early 1720s, were *Roger's Delight*, a popular song written by Thomas D'Urfey, and the traditional folksong *The Fryer well-fitted: or A pretty jest that once befel How a maid put a fryer to cool in the well.*

In the 18th century, ballads in four or five parts, printed on large folio sheets and called 'garlands', were common. See the list of such garlands given by W. J. Ebsworth in the Ballad Society edition of *The Roxburghe Ballads* (9 vols., 1871-99, vol. 8, pp.179ff.), recently issued in an 8-vol. facsimile edition.

With the arrival of the daily newspaper in the 18th century, the urban English tended to lose interest in prose broadsides, which then found refuge in the country inns and farmhouses long after they had been displaced from the city taverns and coffee-houses. The broadside printers, issuing fewer ballad sheets in the 18th century, made up for this in the first sixty years of the 19th century, when John Pitts, James Catnach, and Henry Parker Such (1849-1917) of London dominated a market in which provincial printers also began to claim a share. These provincial printers included Bebbington of Manchester, Harkness of Preston, Walker of Durham, and Marshall of Newcastle. Sharman of Cambridge was Catnach's agent, but I have not so far seen a ballad originally printed by Sharman.

Charles Hindley, in *The life and times of James Catnach* (London, 1878), describes how Catnach, who set up in Monmouth Court in Central London in 1814, paid men to collect ballads from singers in country inns, and at one time kept a fiddler on the premises. Catnach "used to sit receiving ballad-writers and singers, and judging of the merits of any production which was brought to him, by having it sung then and there to some popular air played by his own fiddler, and so that the ballad-singer should be enabled to start at once, not only with the new song, but also the tune to which it was adapted".

The familiar genre of 'sorrowful lamentations' of hanged men is not as ancient as most of the other genres we are examining: it dates from 1820, when there was enacted a law providing for a reasonable lapse of time between a trial and the execution of the guilty party. "Before that", explained a London chaunter to Henry Mayhew, "there wasn't no time for a Lamentation; sentence o' Friday and scraggin' o' Monday. So we only had the Life, Trial and Execution". These were usually prose accounts, possibly with a verse conclusion, as in *THE DYING WORDS and CONFESSION OF Elias Lucas AND Mary Reader* [sic; read Reeder] illustrated here from Cambridge, a broadside 'sorrowful lamentation' and account of the trial which took place before the last public hangings at Cambridge Gaol, in April 1850.

There had been fifteen executions at Cambridge since 1780, when Elizabeth Butchell had been hanged for concealing the birth of a child, but the last had

THE DYING WORDS and CONFESSION OF

Elias Lucas AND Mary Reader,

Who were Executed this morning (April 13) in front of the County Goal at Cambridge, for the wilful MURDER of SUSAN LUCAS.

LIFE, CHARACTER, &c.

The unhappy beings who this day forfeited their lives to the offended laws of their country were brought up in industrious habits and humble circumstances at Castle Camps, about three miles from Haverhill. Lucas was an agricultural labourer, and lived with his wife at the above named village; his partner in crime was his wife's sister, and his victim the wife herself. Lucas was a strong muscular looking man, about 25 years of age, and up to the time of his committing this foul and unnatural crime, bore an excellent character, and was noted for his easy and cheerful disposition. The female was short and plump, and her features were even & good; the expression of her face bore the marks of innocence; her hands were remarkably white and small; and although stated in the calendar to be 20, she seemed not more than 16. Lucas and his wife had been married between 4 and 5 years, and appeared to have lived on excellent terms. The wife's sister lived as servant in Cambridge, to Mr. Miller, a carpenter, residing in Castle End, not far distant from the scene of her trial and melancholy exit; she continued in his service for a period of 15 months, and left on her own accord towards the end of last year, stating that her chest was bad; her master and mistress found no fault with her, and those who lived in the neighbourhood and had opportunities of judging her conduct and character, state that she appeared a well conducted modest girl, and could hardly credit the fact that Ann Reeder, the quiet, good looking, and willing girl they knew so well, could have rushed into a crime so horrible in its nature, so frightful in its effects; She shortly afterwards became servant to Mr. Cross, a farmer in Camps, in whose employ was Lucas. Mr. Cross, it seems, entertained some suspicion there was something wrong between Lucas and his sister-in-law; but no suspicion was entertained by Lucas's wife, for hearing that Mary Reader again complained of illness, Mrs. Lucas invited her sister to live with her, as by paying her attention she thought she could benefit her. Well was that kindness repaid! Well was the unsuspecting victim requited for her sisterly love! Lucas and Mary Reeder not many days after she became an inmate there, planned the poor creature's death. The former had had unfortunately and thoughtlessly by his employer, some poison entrusted to him destroy or make away with; instead of which he took it home, kept it several months, and at length tutored Mary Reeder to place a portion it in a mess of bread and water, which the unsuspecting wife ate for supper. For an account of the agony the poor creature suffered the reader is referred to the report of the trial which follows, and their blood will curdle with horror as they read from those who witnessed the poor wife's death, and the cold-blooded atrocity with which the crime was perpetrated. It will scarcely be believed that hardened man, as he saw his innocent and unsuspecting victim eating the deadly poison, and expressing a disgust at the taste, it being thoroughly seasoned with arsenic, brutally exclaimed to her complaint, "O dall it, mitress, I'll eat mine if it kills me." The brutal joke was understood by his companion in crime; and on his trial there surely never was greater levity displayed by the most hardened criminal than by this man. He frequently turned to laugh at his companions in court; and even when a tin box was brought into court, which held some part of his wife's stomach and intestines, he laughed right out. A few weeks before her death the prisoner's wife was confined; at the time he made an anxious enquiry whether the child was likely to live, and on the nurse remarking it was a fine healthy child, he seemed displeased, and muttered "he hoped it would die." On other occasions he was heard to express a hope that it might not live. That the child did die shortly after its birth is a matter of fact. Mrs. Lucas had 4 children, but only one survives. Lucas accompanied his wife when she went to be churched after her last confinement; on returning to their cottage he seemed absent in thought, at last he said, "wife I have had bad dreams of late; I have dreamed thrice I shall be either hanged or transported; she bade him banish such thoughts from his mind as only tending to make him miserable. It is but just to the memory of the poor woman to state, that she was a good and affectionate wife. The prisoner had never breathed one word against her, but acknowledged she had been a kind, good-hearted, and unsuspecting woman; and he acknowledged more—he has admitted that an improper intimacy had existed between himself and Mary Reader, and which commenced last Christmas, and shortly after her leaving Cambridge and taking up her residence at Cambridge; and that being the case the cause of the murder soon suggests itself. Those who knew Lucas by residing in the same village, and looked upon him as a well-disposed light-hearted young man, can hardly believe him to be guilty of a crime so wicked and monstrous. He would sing and whistle about his employment, and was as blithe and gay as any of the village rustics with whom he companied. Vice, however, triumphed over the ill-fated young man and young woman.—They have this day met a disgraceful death, convicted of the most atrocious crime, by the hands of the common hangman.

TRIAL and CONVICTION.

Elias Lucas, and Mary Reader, were indicted for the wilful murder of Susan Lucas, by administering to her two drachms of arsenic.—Mr. Sanders stated that the prisoners were indicted for the murder of the wife of the male prisoner and the sister of the female prisoner. Lucas had been married about four years to the sister of the other prisoner, who, having left her service at the house of Mr. Cross, near Castle Camps, where Lucas was also employed as an out-door servant, took up her residence at the house of Lucas about the end of January last. About that time it appeared that the deceased who had given birth to three or four children, had been confined, and had lost her child. In the course of a month, however, she had quite recovered, and was in excellent health on the 21st Feb. On the next day she died.—Thomas Reader: I live under the same roof with the prisoners in a double tenement, am uncle to the deceased. I saw the deceased at four o'clock on the 21st. Maria Reeder came to my house next day, and asked me to fetch three penyworth of brandy, for her sister was sick. She gave me the money, and I took it to her. Before I had finished dinner, Maria Reeder called to my wife to come and see her sister, who had fallen out of bed. I went and found the deceased on the floor in the bed room. She was undressed. I helped to put her into bed.—The prisoner Lucas and the deceased seemed to live happily together.—Susan Potter: I was fetched by Thomas Reeder to go to deceased the day she died. She was in bed, and rose up and began to retch violently. She held up her hand, and said, "Elias, go for a doctor." I said so to. He said, "I do, don't I." He left the room immediately: he did not speak to his wife.—Cross examined: He did not stop a minute after she told him to fetch a doctor.—Frederick A. Cramer: I am assistant to Mr. Martin, the surgeon, of Haverhill. On the 22d Feb. Lucas came to me as his wife was dangerously ill. I went, but before I got there was told she was dead. I went to the house, saw Maria Reader. Reeder said, "Sister had been poorly from disease of the chest, had been subject to it some years; they had given her castor oil morning before." She also said they had a mess of water and bread the evening before. Lucas came in and went out again; he said, "She has been very sick—she had complained very much of pain in her chest." I went up to see body; it was warm. I observed she had died in a state of collapse. The fingers were clenched as a bird's claw. Examined the body, found marks of recent confinement. It was supernaturally blue. The symptoms made me think the woman had died from cholera or poison: I suspected the latter. Something was said about a burial. I said I could not account for the death of deceased, and should not give a certificate to the registrar. Maria Reeder said, "To tell you the truth, she has been a deal worse since the water mess last night, and we all think there was something in it which caused her death. Sister complained that it tasted like lime, and offered me some in a spoon. I tasted it, but finding it like what sister described I spit it out. We gave some to the cat, who had also been ill." She also said that her sister 20 minutes after the mess, went to the front door, and, leaning against the sill, vomited into the garden, saying, "I am a dead woman." She never spoke after. She said she had crumbed the mess, and her sister had poured the water upon it. I asked both prisoners whether they had any poisonous substance in the house; both said, "Not they knew of." Went next day and opened the body. The chest was healthy, except some inflammation. I placed the stomach and part of the intestines in a bladder. Went the next day and completed the examination. Asked Lucas if he had ny arsenic in these house—he said he had told Tilbrook (the constable) he had it—it was on the shelf in the back place—that his mistress had given it him to destroy; he shewed it me, I produce it now as I found it. The parcel weighed 16 ounces. Reeder said arsenic could not have got into the basin by accident, for it was on the opposite end of the shelf." I said it was unfortunate for them that arsenic should have been found in the house. Reeder said, "I call God to witness I am innocent of poisoning my sister, though I am aware the world says to that effect.' Alfred Taylor: I found in the stomach water, mucous fluid, and arsenic. There were two grains of metallic arsenic in the stomach, and from the result of my experiments I am prepared to say that death was produced by arsenic given to the deceased in large quantities. Professor Taylor proved that the substance produced in the parcel was arsenic. Mr. Cross proved at the last wheat sowing he gave Lucas nearly a pound of arsenic to destroy. Mr. Justice Wightman (to the witness); For the future I would advise you to take care how you deal with so dangerous an article as that before you. You should have seen it destroyed yourself, and I would caution you against the possession of so large a quantity. Mary Butterfield, was midwife when Susan Lucas was confined. Lucas came in two hours after; he said he wished he was not married, and if he had known what he did then he would not have married her if her father had given her a 1000l." I told him not "to say anything then, as it was a difficult time" This was not in the room where is wife was. He afterwards went to her room and said the same to her, I believe. He then came came down and went out to work. I found his wife crying. On the Sunday after he asked me if the child was like to live or die. I said I thought it did not look like a dying child. I went away on Monday. The deceased had a good getting-up. Mary Butterfield: I am the daughter of the last witness. I went to replace my mother. I stayed till the Saturday. Lucas had eight pigs. I used to feed them. He came home one day in the week and," said He thought his pigs grew well, and he would keep the little cad-pig (the least of the lot) till he married again, and have a green leg of pork for his dinner. He said he should marry this Mary Reader, and went into the house. So did I. He told her he would keep this cad-pig till he married her sister. She said," That would never be, for they never would allow him to marry my sister." He said they can't help themselves, if in case I go a little way from home. Ann Ives heard Lucas say he "wished he could rid of his wife." He did not like a married life. Elizabeth Webb heard him say that his wife "was muddled away in a funny manner.—He said when his wife complained of the mess tasting so bad, he said, "mine is good enough" "D—n it I would eat it if it killed me." He gave the remainder of the mess to eat; she ate some and was sick and bad, but did not die." Mary Carlton went to see deceased on the 26th, and saw Maria Reader in the garden. I was with her father. I said to him, "Is this poor Susan's sister?" She said, "Yes." I hope you do not think me guilty of taking my poor sister's life?" I said, "I hope you are not—but God only knows, I do not; We then went in, and she said "Elias only came home at 10 o'clock last night, and said my case was worse than his, and I said " No; his was worse 'he got the arsenic.' " I said to her, "Why did you not get a doctor for your poor sister?" She said, "He was her husband though; I was her sister." I said to her afterwards in Susannah Reeder's house, "I heard the poor creature was worked upwards and downwards all night." Maria Reeder said, "So she was; if you was to kill me I could not tell you how many times she got up in the night. Not that I know it by seeing her, for I slept at her back at her desire, and slept soundly, and so did Elias." F. Crick,—I went to Mr. Cross's for a sack chaff on the 27th of February. Lucas brought it to me. He said he was in great trouble about his wife. They said she was poisoned, and were agoing to hang him. I said "They cannot hang you if you did not do it." He said that when he wenn he went home he found three water messes, and on his saying he did not like it, his wife said she would put two spoons of sugar in it if he would eat it." He said then he ate his, and when his wife had half eaten hers she said, "Dear me, Elias, my mess tastes very nasty," and with that " she fished and fished about, and and found a gob of arsenic in it." We were alone then. Next day I went to Haverhill with Mr. Cross and Lucas said, "D—n it, master, I'll stand a bottle of gin if I get off this job, to think that I am a single man again; if the girl and I will keep our counsel they cannot hurt us."

Mr. Couch then addressed the jury on behalf of the prisoners; after which the Learned Judge in a clear and able manner summed up the evidence. The Jury after consulting a short period, returned a verdict—GUILTY against both the prisoners. Mr. Justice Wightman, after putting on the black cap, in a solemn and feeling address passed sentence of DEATH on the culprits, urging upon them the necessity of using the short period of time they had to exist in this world in penitence and prayer, and imploring mercy from that Being whose commandments they had broken, and who alone can pardon their transgression.

On hearing sentence pronounced, Lucas (who had conducted himself throughout the trial with the greatest levity) waved his hands, vociferating, "I am not guilty, good bye, ladies and gentlemen. I am innocent."

CONFESSION.

However marked by levity and unconcern the conduct of Lucas during his trial, his deportment after his condemnation underwent a salutary change. Both of these young and unhappy people shortly after leaving the Court became fully sensible of the awful condition their crimes had placed them in, and appeared at once to make up their minds to meet the ignominious punishment that awaited them with penitence and contrition. On finding their fate was inevitable, they both became attentive to their religious duties, and appeared frequently to engage earnestly in prayer—Lucas expressing his sanguine hope and confidence that the Almighty would forgive the crimes he had committed through earnest supplication and repentant prayer. Mary Reader the night after her conviction fully confessed the part she took in the horrible transaction through which herself and her companion in guilt were now about to suffer. She stated, that persuaded by Lucas, she crummed the messes, and, unseen by her sister, conveyed nearly a table-spoon full of arsenic into the basin intended for Mrs. Lucas; but that she now bitterly lamented having been led to commit so great a crime. Lucas for some time persisted in his innocence, and declared that it was not his hand that placed the deadly poison in the basin; but when told of the female's confession—that she had done the act under his direction, he remained silent and appeared quite confounded. He has subsequently confessed to Mr. Orridge, as well those attending upon him in his cell, his participation in and guilty knowledge of the murder. He frequently expressed that he deserved to die, and the sooner the time arrived for his quitting this world the better—and that he felt great hope by praying to his Maker he should be forgiven.

The Condemned Sermon preached on Sunday by the Rev. Mr. Roberts, (in the absence of Mr. Ventris, unable to attend through indisposition) appeared to make a great impression upon both the unhappy culprits. They listened with deep and sorrowful attention to the Rev. gentleman's feeling and admonitory address, and seemed deeply affected throughout the whole of the service.

On Monday the female prisoner was again visited by her father, accompanied by her grandfather, who was much affected at parting, in bidding a last farewell to their wretched and unfortunate offspring. The final parting with her relatives was harrowing in the extreme.

Both the culprits previous to their death acknowledged the justice of their sentence; Lucas frequently repeating, "I deserve to be hanged," "I brought it on myself." Not alone did the wretched man confess the criminal intercourse which had existed between them, but within the last few days his companion in guilt made no scruple in acknowledging that it was that infamous passion which induced her to commit so foul a deed as the murder of an unsuspecting, affectionate, and kind-hearted sister.

The female prisoner a short time before her death (contrary to her former statements) persisted in declaring that Reeder was not aware of her intention to take the life of her sister, and that she alone was implicated in the horrid transaction. She further stated that she had something of importance to communicate which she hoped would not be made public until the moment of her death.

EXECUTION.

Shortly before 12 o'clock the culprits were removed from their cells, when the Executioner commenced the ceremony of pinioning their arms and preparing them for the awful trial they were about to undergo. The mournful cavalcade then slowly proceeded (the chapel bell tolling a solemn sound) towards the platform erected in front of the principal entrance to the goal, which, by the means of a ladder the culprits ascended, accompanied by the Rev. Mr. Roberts, Mr. Orridge governor of the goal, and Calcraft, the well known "finisher of the law." Shortly after the wretched beings were placed under the fatal beam, and after a few moments spent in prayer, the chaplain reading the usual portion of the burial service—the ropes being adjusted, on a signal given the fatal plank fell, and the wretched beings were launched into eternity, in sight of the countless multitude of spectators, who filling the avenues and surrounding the Castle Hill, had assembled to witness the melancholy exit of two youthful criminals who had alike outraged the ties of nature, the laws of their country, and the sacred ordinances of God.

The bodies, after hanging the usual time, on being cut down will be buried within the precincts of the prison.

Seventeen years has elapsed since an execution took place in Cambridge. The last victim to public justice was John Stallon, the Shelford incendiary, who after his condemnation acknowledged being guilty of twelve fires out of thirteen which occurred in that village. Had the severity of the criminal code not been relaxed since that period, from the number of capital offences in the last calendar, we should in all probability have witnessed the melancholy spectacle of more than twenty human beings yielding their lives to the outraged laws of their country.

COPY OF VERSES
Written the night previous to Execution.

O God for mercy we do cry,
To-morrow we are doom'd to die,
Our sins we own are very great,
For which we meet a dreadful fate.

The crime of murder all allow
Is greater than any sin below,
And by the law it is decreed,
On the gallows we shall bleed.

A deadly poison we confess,
We put into our sister's mess,
Hoping when quiet in her grave
More guilty intercourse to have.

God's all-seeing eye doth watch
The actions of the guilty wretch
Wicked deeds he brings to light
Sure as day succeeds the night.

For murder now condemn'd to die
And end our days with infamy,
A crime unequalled to be found,
If you search the world around.

A warning take now by our fate
And shun the evils the [illegible]
A guilty passion which [illegible]
To bring us to this fatal [illegible]

THE DYING WORDS and CONFESSION OF Elias Lucas AND Mary Reader [sic; read Reeder]. Anonymous broadsheet sold in the streets of Cambridge on and after 13 April 1850. No imprint but doubtless a Cambridge sheet. 50 x 38 cm. (*Cambridge and County Folk Museum*) been seventeen years earlier, when John Stallon had been hanged for arson. The *Cambridge Chronicle*, estimating a crowd of 30-40,000, reported in its issue of 20 April 1850:

'Magdalene-street and Castle end were filled with vendors of gallows literature, who dinned into the ears of the lieges the ditties that have done duty on similar occasions (saving the change of names) for the last century. In one group were two vocalists and – a fiddler! and their "copy of verses" began –

"Attend, good people, young and old-
A tale of woe I will unfold;
Of a dreadful murder you shall hear,
At Castle Camps, in Cambridgeshire.

CHORUS.
O What an awful sight to see
Two murderers on the fatal tree", &c. &c.

Another:

"A place well known in Cambridgeshire
Is Castle Camps a village there
Where Mrs Lucas lost her life
A kind and virtuous loving wife", &c. &c.

The vendor of the last was the Indian who, as the dying speech and confession men have it, has "followed the gallows" for a number of years'.

Another Cambridge murder, that of Emma Rolfe by Robert Brown in 1876, was the subject of a Henry Such ballad written to the tune 'Driven from home'.

Broadsides dealing with murder can be classified into two types: the ballad slip, like 'A Copy of Verses COMPOSED ON THE HORRID MURDER, At Stukely'; and the catchpenny prose account, often (as in the Manning example also illustrated) accompanied by a ballad moralizing on the events in a more general way.

The village of Stukely, near Huntingdon (now in Cambridgeshire), was the scene of the murder of the Rev. Joshua Waterhouse by Joshua Slade on 3 July 1827, and this ballad must have been composed shortly after Slade's hanging on 1 September 1827. Though there is no imprint, an early hand has attributed the ballad slip to S. Wilson of Bridge Street, who printed it as was usual with another slip to form a broadside, in this case probably several years later. Neither of the woodcuts is remotely apposite, again a characteristic of the mass-produced broadside, and Wilson could find no other local slip to join with the Stukely ballad, so he added a comic ballad of a West Country farmer.

Late in 1850, Henry Mayhew interviewed a London street-patterer who specialized in selling execution broadsheets and had travelled East Anglia

A Copy of Verses
COMPOSED ON THE
HORRID MURDER,
At Stukely.

By S. S.

Come all you wild and wicked youths and lend a silent ear
Unto these melancholy lines that I have written here,
Its of a dreadful murder the truth I will unfold,
The bare recital of the tale will make your blood run cold.

It was at Little Stukely near Huntingdon so fair,
One Joshua Slade he did reside as you shall quickly hear,
A young man only 18 years just in the prime of life,
And for the crime of murder he has forfeited his life.

It was on the 3d of July this murderous deed was done,
At the Vicarage House at Stukely near to Huntingdon,
The Rev. Joshua Waterhouse he did reside alone,
Who murdered was by Slade's own hand he now does fairly own.

The body of the Gentleman in a large tub was found,
Which kept the blood which fast did flow from running on the ground,
The wretched victim as we hear a lifeless corpse was found,
And soon the tidings of the same was spread the country round.

Then Joshua Slade he taken was and unto prison sent,
Until the Assizes he did lay his crime for to lament,
At length arraigned at the bar he forced was to stand,
Where blood for blood it is required by the law of God & man.

When the jury found him guilty it to him was made known,
But still unto the murder he never then would own,
The judge in passing sentence made him this reply,
You're guilty, Joshua Slade, so prepare yourself to die,

Of all the crimes recorded in history from the first,
The horrid crime of murder it is the very worst,
To murder this old gentleman whose life to him was dear,
'Twould fill the eye of sympathy with many a flowing tear.

It was September the first day this young man he did die,
All for this cruel murder upon the gallows high,
The wages of sin is certain death, to all he loud did say.
But the gift of God is eternal life,---farewell and for me pray.

May the Lord have mercy on his soul, have mercy Lord we pray,
When he appears before the throne at the great judgement day
May he be numbered with thy flock and happy may he be,
And praise thy name for evermore to all eternity.

The KING
AND THE
West Countryman.

There was an old chap in the west country,
A flaw in his lease the Lawyer found,
'Twas all about selling of five Oak trees,
And building a house upon his own ground.

Now this old chap to Lunnun would go,
To tell the King a part of his woe,
Likewise to tell him part of his grief,
In hopes King George would give him relief.

When this old chap to Lunnun had come,
And found the King to Windsor had gone,
He said if he'd known he'd be from home,
He dang'd his buttons if ever he'd come.

Now this old chap to Windsor did stump,
The gates were barred and all secure,
He knock'd and thumpt with his Oaken clump,
There's room in here for I to be sure.

But when he got there lord how he did stare,
To see the yeoman a strutting about,
He scratch'd his head and rubb'd down his hair,
In the ears of the Nobles he gave a great shout,

Pray Mr. Noble shew I the King,
Be that the King that I see there,
I zee'd a chap at Bartlemy fair,
Look'd more like a King than that chap there.

Pray Mr. King and how do you do,
I'ze gotten for you a bit of a job,
Which if you will be so kind as to do,
I'ze gotten a summut for you in my fob.

The King he took the lease in hand,
To sign it he was likewise willing,
The Farmer to make him a bit of amends,
He pull'd out his purse and gave him a shilling.

The King to carry on the joke,
Ordered ten pounds to be laid down,
The Farmer stared but nothing spoke,
But stared again and scratch'd his crown.

The cash made the Farmer look wond'rous funny
To pick it up he was likewise willing,
He said if he'd known he'd got so much money,
Dang'd his buttons if he'd gee'd him a shilling.

A Copy of Verses composed on the Horrid Murder, At Stukely. By S.S. Broadside ballads printed *c*. 1830 by S. Wilson, Bridge St., Cambridge though without imprint. Type & ornaments 22½ x 17 cm. (*Cambridge University Library, Madden Collection*) during the previous year, earning his living principally from the murder of Patrick O'Connor by Frederick and Maria Manning. The penny broadsheet on the execution on 13 November 1849 was so popular that the returns for the total sales of copies of this broadsheet alone, as estimated by Mayhew, was 2,500,000, and a like sale was estimated for the Rush broadsheet. The bulk of these broadsheets (though not all) were printed in London and the majority sold in the provinces, including Cambridge. Reckoning that each copy was sold for 1d. (patterers objected to selling 7 popular sheets for 6d.), the money expended on the six best-selling broadsheets on murderers amounted to £48,500 in one year.

Mayhew's patterer, speaking of his trade in Rush and Manning broadsheets, reminisced: "Irish Jem, the Ambassador [a fellow-patterer], never goes to bed but he blesses Rush the farmer; and many's the time he told me we should never have such another windfall as that. But I told him not to despair; there's a good time coming, boys, says I, and, sure enough, up comes the Bermondsey tragedy. We might have done very well, indeed, out of the Mannings, but there was too many examinations for it to be any great account to us. I've been away with the Mannings in the country ever since. I've been through Hertfordshire, Cambridgeshire, and Suffolk, along with George Frederic Manning and his wife – travelled from 800 to 1,000 miles with 'em, but I could have done much better if I had stopped in London . . .".

A patterer selling street literature between London and Birmingham commonly reached Cambridge via Romford, Chelmsford, Braintree, Thaxted and Saffron Walden, paying 3d. to 4d. a night (at slack times for a bed to himself) in the better lodging-houses, or at the busier times (during fairs or race-meetings) for *any* share in one of lower quality.

"Yorkshire Betty's is the head quarters at Cambridge, – or in Barnwell, of course, there's no such places in Cambridge. It's known as 'W——— and Muck Fort'. It's the real college touch – the seat of learning, if you're seeing life. The college lads used to look in there oftener than they do now. They're getting shyer. Men won't put up with black eyes for nothing. Old Yorkshire Betty's a motherly body, but she's no ways particular in her management. Higgledy-piggledy; men and women; altogether". To which account of Yorkshire Betty's 'padding-ken' or lodging-house, Mayhew himself adds laconically 'Thirty beds'.

Getting down to business, the London patterer enjoyed a steady sale of his broadsheets in Cambridge: "The grand town of all. London in miniature. It would be better but for the police. I don't mean the college bull-dogs. They don't interfere with us, only with women. The last time I was at Cambridge, sir, I hung the Mannings. It was the day, or two days, I'm not sure which, after their trial. We pattered at night, too late for the collegians to come out. We 'worked' about where we knew they lodged – I had a mate with me – and some of the windows of their rooms, in the colleges themselves, looks into the street. We pattered about later news of Mr and Mrs Manning. Up went the windows, and cords was let down to tie the papers to. But we

A Long-Song Seller or ballad vendor, *c*. 1849. From a daguerrotype by Beard in Henry Mayhew, *London labour and the London poor,* 1861, vol.1, p.273.

The Street-Stationer. *c*. 1849. From a daguerrotype by Beard in Henry Mayhew, *London labour and the London poor*, 1861, vol.1, p.297.

A COPY OF VERSES
Humbly presented to the Right Worshipful the
MAYOR
The ALDERMEN, and COMMON COUNCIL-MEN,
And the rest of my worthy Masters and Mistresses, dwelling in *Cambridge*,
By SAMUEL SAUL, BELL-MAN, 1780.

Bellman's Verses, 1780.
Broadside 53½ x 39 cm.
(*Cambridgeshire Collection*)

COPY OF VERSES
HUMBLY PRESENTED
BY THE
Lamplighters of Cambridge,
1867.

Lamplighter's Verses, 1867.
Broadside 29 x 22 cm.
(*Cambridgeshire Collection*)

always had the money first. We weren't a-going to trust such out-and-out going young coves as them. One young gent. said: 'I'm a sucking parson; won't you trust *me*?'. 'No', says I, 'we'll not trust Father Peter'. So he threw down 6d. and let down his cord, and he says, 'Send six up'. We saw it was Victoria's head all right, so we sends up three. 'Where's the others?', says he. 'O', says I, 'they're 1d. a piece, and 1d a piece extra for hanging Mr and Mrs Manning, as we have, to a cord; so it's all right'. Some laughed, and some said, 'D———n you, wait till I see you in the town'. But they hadn't that pleasure".

Another common type of broadside was the bellman's ballad. John Stow, in *A Survay* [sic] *of London* (1598), described the bellmen of his time "going round the parish with a bell, and at every lane's end, and at the ward's end, giving warning of fire or candle, and to help the poor and pray for the dead".

"It seems to have been customary", one reads in Robert Chambers' *Book of days* (vol. 1 of 2, 1863, p.497), "for the Bellman to go about at a certain season of the year, probably Christmas, amongst the householders of his district, giving each a copy of his broadside – firing a broadside at each, as it were – and expecting from each in return some small gratuity, as an addition to his ordinary salary. The execrable character of his poetry is indicated by the contempt with which the wits speak of 'bellman's verses'.

The bellman's functions varied from town to town, and from time to time. Thus, he could perform the functions of watchman, town-crier, postman, or (with sandwich-boards or bell) advertising man. In Cambridge (Cooper's *Annals,* vol. 4, p.195), the duties of bellman were combined with those of a town crier in 1727. Thirty years later the first Cambridge bellman's verse was printed, the bellman being Samuel Saul until 1786. Thomas Adams took over in 1787, issuing his last broadside in 1819. In 1820 Isaac Moule Jr. became bellman, dying in office on 18 February 1854 at the age of 77, and apparently no more sheets were issued. The Cambridgeshire Collection has the bellman's verses of Cambridge for the years 1780 [illustrated here], 1786, 1805, 1810, 1815, 1816, 1819, 1822, 1825, 1826, 1828, 1829, 1830 and 1831.

Much of the style and content of their verses was plagiarised or adapted by provincial bellmen from London sheets, but one often finds references to local personalities, or to Cambridge events which were fitted into the usual framework.

Lamplighters then took a leaf out of the bellmen's book handing out broadsides in exchange for a Christmas gratuity. A copy of verses by the Cambridge lamplighters is illustrated here for comparison. The Cambridgeshire Collection possesses lamplighter's verses for 1851, 1853, 1855, 1867 and 1869, the first two without imprint and the last three printed by Wilson & Son.

The comic ballad *The Literary Dustman*, printed in the 1830s by Henry Talbot of Cambridge, belongs to a popular genre associated with the development of music-hall and the humorous monologue written for stage performance.

The Crampton and Baring-Gould collections of broadsides in the British Library are, like the Harding Collection in the Bodleian, mounted on sheets and unclassified, offering a wealth of material for those with unlimited time at their disposal.

So far uncatalogued, for Harding died in 1973 and the Bodleian acquired his collection as recently as 1974, a 3-volume set of *Ballads & Songs,* totalling more than two thousand ballad slips, is devoted to sheets issued between about 1790 and 1840. None of these appears to have been printed at Cambridge, but there are two interesting Cambridge association-items. On p.145 there is a slip entitled *The Cambridge Ghost; or, the Scrag of Mutton. A Parody on Giles Scroggins. Sung at the Lyceum.* With a woodcut of mistress and maid in a kitchen, the slip bears the imprint 'Printed and sold by J. Jennings, no. 5 Water-Lane, Fleet St '. Between pp.207 and 208, bearing neither place of printing nor printer's name, is the ballad slip *The Cruel Father*, illustrated with a more than usually crude woodcut of a longnosed plug-ugly. The ballad opens:

"In Cambridge fair city a rich damsel did dwell,
For wit and for beauty few could her excel;
Her name was Diana scarce fifteen years old
Her portion was twelve thousand pounds in gold,
Besides an estate when her father did die . . ."

Cambridge University Library has the Harmsworth Collection, eight vols. of late-19th century ballad-sheets and slips collected initially by A.M. Broadley, and the Sir Frederick Madden Collection of more than 17,500 broadside ballads (mainly 1775-1850) in 26 vols. Madden's Cambridge imprints are [Wilson] of Bridge Street (11 examples); 'Talbot and Ladds, Sussex-st.' (one example); and H. Talbot, Sussex-street' (29 examples) all with a rectangular ruled border except for a mid-1830s unillustrated sheet including *The Amphitrite* (on a convict ship lost off 'Bologne' in a gale on 31 August 1833) and *Umbrella Courtship*. The other broadside ballads 'Printed and Sold by H. Talbot, Sussex-street, Cambridge' which can be seen in the Madden Collection are:

1. 'Allow'd to be Drunk on the Premises' (with a woodcut of a sly sailor); 'Rise, Gentle Moon'; and 'Where the Bee Sucks'.
2. 'Betsy Of Deptford And her Young Sailor Bold' (with a fleuron); 'The Drover Boy' (with a bull woodcut); and 'Trim the Lamp'.
3. 'Black Eye'd Susan' (with an anchor woodcut); and 'Unhappy Jeremiah' (with a woodcut of a jovial farmhand holding a pitchfork beside a tree).
4. 'Blow the candle in' (with a fleuron); and 'Love and Liver'.
5. 'Death of Lord Nelson' (with woodcut of 'Lord Nelson' between flags); 'Young Edwin in the Lowlands Low'.
6. 'Dream of Napoleon' (with woodcut of Chinese scene set in ornamental border); 'How, When, and Where' (with nuts woodcut); and 'The Banks of the Blue Moselle' (with fleuron).
7. 'The Farmer's Boy' (with woodcut of sailor, bust-length, as used also on 'The Female Cabin Boy', illustrated); and 'The Poor Little Fisherman's Girl' (with framed woodcut of an angler standing in a river).
8. 'The Farmer's Daughter, and the Gay Plough-Boy' (with a woodcut of an aristocratic lady in lowcut evening dress, with choker); 'The Streamlet'; and 'Awake! on your Hills'.
9. 'The Female Smuggler' (with the same anchor woodcut as used also on no. 3 above; and 'Jonathan Brown' (with a framed woodcut of an old man supported by a walking-stick).
10. 'Flora, the Lily of the West' (with woodcut of Chinese scene different from that in no. 6 above); and 'She was Such a Nice Young Gal' (with a woodcut showing a bent crone with walking-stick holding out her hand towards the outstretched hand of a youth in wrong perspective).
11. 'The Grand Conversation on Napoleon' (with a woodcut of a bare-breasted classical heroine clutching an upturned pillar); and 'The Brave Old Oak' (with the royal arms).

THE

Literary DUSTMAN.

H. TALBOT, PRINTER, SUSSEX-STREET, CAMBRIDGE.

SOME folks may boast of sense, egad !
  Vot holds a lofty station ;
But tho' a dustman, I have had
  A lib'ral *hedecashun*.
And tho' I never vent to school,,
  Like many of my betters,
A turnpike-man. vot varnt no fool,
  He larnt me all my letters.
They calls me Adam Bell, ' tis clear,
  As Adam vos the fust man,—
And by a co-in-side-ance queer,
  Vy I'm the fust of Dustmen,
  Vy I'm the fust of Dustmen !

At sartin schools they makes boys write,
  Their alphabet on sand, sirs,
So, I thought dust vould do as vell,
  And larnt it out of hand. sirs ;
Took in the " Penny Magazine,"
  And Johnson's *Dixonary*:
And all the Peri o-di-cals,
  To make me *literary*. They calls, &c.

My dawning genus fust did peep.
  Near Battle bridge 'tis plain, sirs,
You recollect the cinder heap,
  Vot stood in Gray's-Inn-lane, sirs?
'Twas there I studied pic-turesque,
  Vhile I my bread vos yearnin';
And there inhalin' the fresh breeze,
  I *sifted out my lernin* ! They calls, &c.

Then Mrs. Bell twixt you and I,
  Vould melt a heart of stone, sirs,
To hear her pussy's wittals cry,
  In such a *barrow tone*, sirs ;
My darters all take arter her,
  In grace and figure easy ;
They larns to sing, and as they're fat,
  I has 'em taught by *Grisi* ! They calls, &c.

Ve dines at four, and arter that,
  I smokes a mild *Awanna* ;
Or gives a lesson to the lad,
  Upon the grand *pianna*
Or vith the gals valk a *quod-rille*,
  Or takes a cup of coffee ;
Or, if I feels fatig'd or ill,
  I lounges on the *sophy*. They calls, &c.

Or arter dinner read a page
  Of Valter Scott, or Byron ;
Or Mr. Shikspur. on the stage,
  Subjects none can tire on.
At night ve toddles to the play,
  But not to gallery attic ;
Drury-Lane's the time o' day,
  And quite *aristocratic* !

I means to buy my eldest son
  A comission in the Lancers,
And makes my darters every one,
  Accomplished Hopra dancers.
Great sculptors all conwarse wi' me,
  And call my taste diwine, sirs,
King George's *statty* at Kings's Cross,
  Vos built from my design, sirs! They calls, &c

And Ven I'm made a member on,
  For that I means to try, sirs,
Mr. Gully fought his vay.
  And verefore shou'dn't I, sirs?
Yes, vhen I sits in Parli'ment,
  In old Sin Stephen's College,
I means to take, tis my intent,
  The " Taxes off o' knowledge."
They calls me Adam Bell, 'tis true,
  Cause Adam was the fust man
I'm sure it's very plain to you.
  I'm a *litterary dustman*.

The Soldier who Died for his King.

DEAR maid of my soul ! should I perish
  Where battle's rude discord speaks loudly
The name of thy fond lover cherish,
  And let thy young bosom beat proudly.
My own banner over me wave.
  My broken shield over me fling;
And carve on the oak o'er my grave---
  The soldier who died for his king!"

Yet, maid, when my life-blood is streaming
  One tear to my last moment given,
Like a star in thy blue eyes beaming,
  To me were a foretaste of heaven!
My own banner over me wave,
  My broken shield over me fling;
And carve on the oak o'er my grave---
  The soldier who died for his king!"

The Literary Dustman. Anonymous broadside ballads printed *c.* 1835 by Henry Talbot, Sussex St., Cambridge. Borders 22 x 15 cm. (*Cambridge University Library, Madden Collection*)

12. 'Jim Crow' (with a woodcut of a jovial farmhand identical to that used also on no. 3 above); and 'After Many Roving Years'.
13. 'The Literary Dustman' (with the same woodcut of an old man with walking-stick as on no. 10 above); and 'The Soldier who Died for his King' (with the same fleuron as on no. 4 above).
14. 'Little Town's Boy' (with coat-of-arms blank save close horizontal lines); and 'Captain Ross'.
15. 'Missee Jim Crow' (with a woodcut of a dancing negress); and 'The Soldier's Tear'.
16. 'Mr. Ferguson, It's All Very Fine, But you don't lodge here' (with a woodcut of a printing press); and 'The Light Of Other Days'.
17. 'Phoebe: The Beauty of Dundee' (with the same bare-breasted classical heroine as on no. 11 above); 'The Fine Old English Gentleman'; and 'My Native Higland [sic] Home'.
18. 'The Pirate's Bride, or, Good Bye my Love' (with the same aristocratic lady in lowcut evening dress as in no. 8 above); and 'Steam! Steam!' (with two small woodcuts, one of a bellows and the other of a wheeled engine[?]).
19. 'Pretty Susan, the Pride of Kildare' (with the same aristocratic lady in lowcut evening dress as in nos. 8 and 18 above); and 'The Mistletoe Bough' (with the same nuts woodcut as in no. 6 above).
20. 'The Rambling Sailor' (with the same sailor woodcut as on no. 1 above); and 'I wonder where the Money Goes!'.
21. 'The Rose of Britain's Isle'; 'The Gipsy Prince' (with a coat-of-arms woodcut); and 'My Pretty Jane' (with the same fleuron as on no. 6 above).
22. 'They Say I'm too Little For any thing'; 'Harry Bluff' (with the same anchor woodcut as on nos. 3 and 9 above, but here reversed left to right); and 'Banks of Allan Water'.
23. 'Undaunted Mary, on the Banks of Sweet Dundee'; and 'Little Mary the Sailor's Bride' (with a woodcut showing the tearful farewell of a young lady to a departing sailor, a manned boat at left awaiting the latter).
24. 'When Fair Susan I Left' (with the same farewell woodcut as on no. 23 above); 'The Swiss Boy' (with fleuron); and 'The Female Cabin Boy' (with the same woodcut on 'The Farmer's Boy', no. 7 above).
25. 'Will Watch, the Bold Smuggler' (with the same farewell woodcut as on no. 23 above); 'The Canadian Boat Song' (with fleuron); and 'Some Love to Roam' (with fleuron).
26. 'A Woman, Dear Woman, for me'; and 'The Gallant Sailor, and Nobleman's Daughter'.
27. 'Young Edward, the Gallant Hussar' (with woodcut of stagecoach and horses); 'The Old Miser'; and 'The Sweet Silver Light Bonny Moon'.
28. 'Young Napoleon, or the Bonny Bunch of Roses, O'; 'Isle of Beauty, Fare Thee Well' (with lyre and trumpet); and 'Alice Gray'.

WHEN FAIR SUSAN

I LEFT.

Printed & Sold by H. TALBOT, Sussex Street, Cambridge.

WHEN fair SUSAN I left with a heart full of woe,
And to sea went, my fortune to mend.
Her soft swelling bosom beat hard to and fro,
When she lost both her love and her friend.
'Fare thee well, Tom!' she cry'd, and bid me adieu,
While the tears ran' in showers from her eyes,
I sail'd full of grief to join the ship's crew,
While loud waves to my sorrow replies.

The winds they blew hard, and seas 'gan to roar,
While blue lightning around us did flash,
I thought of my Susan and wish'd me on shore.
Still the waves most tremendous did dash.
At length a leak sprung, and all hands call'd on deck
In vain every art try'd to save,
I swam on a plank and escaped from the wreck,
The rest met a watery grave.

Kind fortune having thus preserved my life,
To my Susan I thought I would go,
With joy I should meet with my long absent wife,
But hopes were all changed into woe.
For the news reach'd her ears that the ship it was lost,
And Thomas her love was no more,
She died like a rose when nipt by the frost,
And I live, her loss to deplore.

The Swiss Boy.

Come arouse thee, arouse thee, my brave Swiss boy
Take thy pail and to labour away,
The sun is up with ruddy beam.
The Kine are thronging to the stream,
Come arouse thee, arose thee, my brave Swiss boy,
Take thy pail and to labour away.

Am not I, am not I, say, a merry Swiss boy!
When I hie to the mountain away:
For there a shepherd maiden dear
Awaits my song with list'ning ear,
Am not I, am not I, then, a merry Swiss boy,
When I hie to the mountain away?

Then at night, then at night, Oh! a gay Swiss boy,
I'm away to my comrades away,
The cup we fill, the wine is pass'd
In friendship round, until at last,
With 'Good night' and 'Good night' the happy Swiss boy
To his home and his slumbers away.

THE FEMALE

CABIN BOY.

Printed and Sold by H. TALBOT, Sussex Street, Cambridge.

It is of a pretty female as you shall understand,
She had a mind for roving unto a foreign land,
Attired in sailor's clothing she boldly did appear,
And engaged with the captain to serve him for one year.
She engaged with the captain as cabin boy to be,
The wind it was in favour, so they put out to sea,
The captain's lady being on board, she seemed to enjoy
So glad the captain had engaged the handsome cabin boy.

So nimble was that pretty maid, & done her duty well,
But mark what followed after, the song itself will tell
The captain with that pretty maid did oftimes kiss and toy
For he soon found out the secret of the female cabin boy.
Her cheeks appear'd like roses, and with her side locks curled,
The sailors of'times smiled and said, he's just like a girl,
But eating captain's biscuit her color did destroy,
And the waist did swell of pretty Nell, the female cabin boy

As thro' the Bay of Biscay their gallant ship did plough,
One night among the sailor's there was a pretty row,
They bundled from their hammocks, it did their rest destroy,
And they swore about the groaning of the handsome cabin boy.
O doctor, oh doctor, the cabin boy did cry,
The sailors swore by all was good, the cabin boy would die,
The doctor ran with all his might, and smiling at the fun,
To think a sailor lad should have a daughter for a son.

The sailors, when they heard the joke, they all began to stare,
The child belong'd to none of them they solemnly did swear,
The lady to the captain said, my dear I wish you joy,
It's either you or I betray'd the female cabin boy.
So they all took up a bumper, & drank success to trade,
And likewise to the cabin boy, though neither man nor maid,
And if the waves should rise again, the sailors to destroy,
Why we then must ship some sailors like the handsome cabin boy.

WHEN FAIR SUSAN I LEFT. Anonymous ballad slips printed as a broadside *c*. 1830 by Henry Talbot, Sussex St., Cambridge. Borders 22½ x 16½ cm. (*Cambridge University Library, Madden Collection*)

The crudity of the woodcuts is reminiscent of those of the Middle Ages, and indeed a number of blocks, left in a drawer or mislaid, could well survive many decades, and reappear not much the worse for wear in contexts wildly (and often uproariously) inappropriate to that for which they had been originally intended. Though all of the blocks on the Talbot and Wilson ballads were *printed* from at a date later than 1800, they were almost all certainly *made* earlier than 1800 for, as Bliss states, wood engraving was developed about 1800, and largely superseded woodcutting thereafter*.

* Douglas Percy Bliss, *A history of wood-engraving* (London, 1928), p.2.

Cambridgeshire Cameos.

XXVIII.—Cambridge Gaols. I.

PREVIOUS to the erection of Queen Anne Terrace facing the South side of Parker's Piece, the site was occupied by a gaol, the last of those which were exclusively for the Borough of Cambridge. History mentions three such gaols. The first of these was the old Tolbooth near the Market Place; and its record opens with a curious statement which might be mistaken for fiction, were it not duly authenticated by the historian. Fuller, in his "History of Cambridge," under date of A.D. 1224 (8 Hen. III.) says: "The King by his letters to the Sheriff of Cambridgeshire gave order that he should put the bailiffs of Cambridge into the possession of the house of Benjamin the Jew (probably forfeited to the Crown on his misdemeanour) to make thereof a common gaol for their Corporation." This house is traditionally identified with the old Tolbooth near the Market Place, of which Carter thus writes in 1753: "The Town Gaol adjoining the Town Hall is a most shocking place to be confined in, especially for food, lodging, and air, all of which are very indifferent." The gaoler was allowed to sell ale to the prisoners, and his appreciation of this perquisite is evidenced by the following note from the *Annals* (iv. 440): "On the 30th of April, 1789, John Doggett, the gaoler, presented a petition to the Justices in which he stated that the profits from the gaoler's former privilege of selling ale were considered a reasonable allowance for keeping the Gaol." A new Gaol having been built in 1788 on a part of the Hobson estate, at the back of the Spinning House, the old Tolbooth was demolished in 1790, in accordance with the following advertisement which is from the *Cambridge Chronicle*, January 30, of that year:—

CAMBRIDGE TOWN GAOL.

TO be SOLD by AUCTION, at the White Bear inn, in Cambridge, on Saturday, the 6th day of February next, between the hours of three and five in the afternoon, subject to such conditions as will be there and then produced;

All that MESSUAGE or TENEMENT and BUILDING, situate near the Shire-hall in the said Town, late in the occupation of John Doggett and used as the Town Gaol.

Which said premises will be either conveyed in fee, or demised for 999 years under the annual rent of a pepper corn, at the option of the purchaser.

By order,
ROBERT WHITE, Town Clerk.

CAMBRIDGE, 28th Jan., 1790.

URBS CAMBORITUM.

FOISTER & JAGG PRINTERS CAMBRIDGE.

Cambridgeshire Cameos, XXVIII – Cambridge Gaols. I. Broadsheet undated but *c.* 1920 printed by Foister & Jagg in Cambridge. One of a series by 'Urbs Camboritum' i.e. W.R. Brown. 29 x 22½ cm. (*Author's Collection*)

Mems. and Gems of Old Cambridge Lore.

JOHN NICHOLSON, *alias* "Maps."

JOHN NICHOLSON, who is known to fame by the nick-name "MAPS," was a bookseller and stationer in Cambridge from 1752 to 1796. This nick-name was a second-hand one, being originally applied to Robert Watts, who started the first circulating library in Cambridge. It is said that this worthy on his rounds used to announce himself at his customers' doors by calling out "MAPS," and this naturally enough accounts for his being thus conventionally designated. He died on January 31st, $175\frac{1}{2}$,* and left his stock-in-trade to his only daughter. She very shortly afterwards married John Nicholson, who thus acquired the business and the circulating library with his father-in-law's nickname in the bargain. A Greek hexameter thus commemorates this sobriquet :—

ΜΑΠΣ *αὐτὸν καλέουσι θεοί, ἄνδρες δέ Νιχολσον,*

Of this the following may be taken as a free and easy version :—

The 'Varsity Gods, they call him MAPS ;
He's Nicholson to other chaps.

Nicholson himself preferred a more grandiloquent form of his own elaboration :—

MAPPESIANI BIBLIOPOLII CUSTOS.

His shop was one of a row of old-fashioned houses which blocked the east end of King's College, it was nearly opposite to St. Edward's passage—there it was that his father-in-law lived before him, and there Nicholson lived and carried on the business until his death in August, 1796. His son succeeded him in the business, which continued to be carried on in the same house until 1807, when he removed it to a house on Senate House Hill, the premises now occupied by Messrs. Macmillan and Bowes.

URBS CAMBORITUM.

* That is 1751, according to the *legal* method of reckoning ; and 1752, according to the ordinary chronology ; both systems were in vogue at that time.

FOISTER & JAGG, PRINTERS, CAMBRIDGE.

Mems and Gems of Old Cambridge. John Nicholson, *alias* "Maps". Broadsheet by 'Urbs Camboritum' (W.R. Brown) printed *c.* 1920 by Foister & Jagg in Cambridge. 28½ x 22 cm. (*Author's Collection*)

The 20th-century broadsheet series 'Leaflets of Local Lore', 'Cambridgeshire Cameos', and 'Mems. and Gems of Old Cambridge Lore' were compiled mostly by W.R. Brown, writing as 'Urbs Camboritum', and printed mainly by Foister and Jagg, originally in Petty Cury, but now in Abbey Walk, who have no early records of their own.

The Oleander Press began its own series of 'Cambridgeshire Broadsheets' in 1976, with Rigby Graham's drawing of Swaffham Prior Windmill, and continued with a sheet to celebrate the centenary of Heffer's Bookshop, and with Peter Jeevar's drawing of Haslingfield dovehouse, all locally printed by The Burlington Press at Foxton in limited editions.

Further Reading

Ashton, John. *A century of ballads.* Detroit, 1968. [Following the original edition of 1887].

Blagden, Cyprian. 'Notes on the ballad market in the second half of the seventeenth century'. In *Papers of the Bibliographical Society of the University of Virginia,* vol. 6, 1953-4. [Though this deals with London printers, there is much that a student of Cambridge printing can learn from the discussion of techniques and traffic in early ballad printing]

Bratton, J.S. *The Victorian popular ballad.* London, 1975.

Child, F.J. *The English and Scottish popular ballads.* 5 vols. New York, 1965. [Following the original Boston edition (5 vols.) of 1882-98. This is the basic source material for a comprehensive view of the field, with useful introductory essays, though Child did not live to produce the analytical study which he was qualified to write]

Friedman, Albert B. *The Penguin book of folk ballads of the English-speaking world.* Harmondsworth, 1977. [This is the work hitherto known as *The Viking book of folk ballads of the English-speaking world*]

Goodman, J. *ed. Bloody versicles: the rhymes of crimes.* Newton Abbot, 1971.

Hindley, Charles. *Curiosities of street literature.* London, 1871. [There is a new edition in 2 vols. published in 1966 by John Foreman, 'The Broadsheet King', 15 Mortimer Terrace, London N.W.5]

Holloway, John *and* Black, Joan. *eds. Later English broadside ballads.* London, 1975. [Interesting particularly because of the fact that all 127 examples are drawn from the Madden Collection in Cambridge University Library]

Kidson, Frank. 'The ballad sheet and garland'. In *Journal of the English Folk-Song Society,* no. 7, 1905.

Marshburn, J.H. *Murder and witchcraft in England, 1550-1640, as recounted in pamphlets, ballads, broadsides and plays* Norman, Okla., 1971.

Pinto, V. de Sola *and* Rodway, A.E. *eds. The common muse: popular British ballad poetry from the 15th to the 20th century.* Harmondsworth, 1965.

Rollins, Hyder E. 'The black-letter broadside ballad'. In *PMLA,* vol. 34 (1919), p.260.

Rollins, Hyder E. *The pack of Autolycus, or Strange and terrible news . . . as told in broadside ballads of the years 1624-1693.* Cambridge, Mass., 1927.

Rollins, Hyder E. *ed. The Pepys Ballads.* 8 vols. Cambridge, Mass., 1929-32.

Shepard, Leslie. *The broadside ballad: a study in origins and meanings.* London, 1962.

Shepard, Leslie. *John Pitts, ballad printer of Seven Dials, London, 1765-1844.* Private Libraries Association, Ravelston, South View Road, Pinner, 1963. [No direct reference to Cambridge, but Pitts was the chief rival to the legendary ballad printer Jemmy Catnach; productions of both were sold throughout Cambridgeshire and the rest of England]

Stokes, Henry Paine. 'The Cambridge bellmen'. In *Procs. Cambridge Antiquarian Soc.*, vol. 14, 1915-16, pp.33-39.

Chapbooks and Religious Tracts

Towards the end of the 17th century, the popularity of the black-letter broadside ballad was decreasing. "There was, of course", writes Blagden, "no nice clean ending; it guttered out in the stronger light of the 18th-century chapbook".

A chapbook is a 'cheap book' (hence the name) produced from a broadside sheet folded into four pages (quarto), eight (octavo), twelve (duodecimo), or sixteen (sixteenmo), and generally sold uncut and unstitched. The buyers, who did not want more substantial books, or could not afford them, then used to cut the pages, and either pin or stitch them together.

Their subject matter was more varied than that of broadside ballads, for in addition to songs and verses, the chapbooks told adventure stories, fairy tales, jokes, riddles, sermons, and even 'histories' that were however a mish-mash of the imagined and the traditional anecdote with never a pretence at scholarship. They were carried by pedlars, also known as 'chapmen', who wandered the countryside, where shops were scarce, with ribbons, pins, needles, thimbles and similar goods for the country wives.

Priced at a penny (or less, if times were hard for the chapmen), the chapbooks formed – with the Bible and the occasional ballad broadside and almanack – the staple reading matter of the English countryman from the late 17th century to the early 19th. The jest-book and ballad were popular in Elizabethan times, but such trifles were suppressed during the Commonwealth, when political and religious tracts came to be dominant. From the time of the Restoration, the bitter controversies dividing the land began to diminish, and the popular chapbook came into its own, often illustrated with crude woodcuts so often reused that by about 1810 they had become almost unrecognisable.

An 'Acte for the punishment of vacabondes* issued in the reign of Elizabeth I links chapmen with Cambridge in a disreputable context: "It ys nowe publyshed that . . . all ydle persones going aboute in any countrey of the said Realme, using subtyll craftye and unlawfull games or playes, and some of them fayning themselves to have knowledge in phisnomye, palmestrye, . . . all juglers, pedlars, tynkers, and petye chapmen . . . and all scollers of the Universityes of Oxford or Cambridge y^{t} goe about begginge . . .

* 14 Eliz. ch. v. 'Statutes', vol. iv, part i. p.155

shalbee deemed roges vacabounds and sturdy beggers intended of by this present act".

In V.E. Neuburg's *Chapbooks: a bibliography,* Cambridge is not represented, though Neuburg states that between 1720 and 1770 "most of the chapbooks printed in England came from the Dicey press, and their productions were printed clearly on good paper, with woodcut illustrations". So, since Dicey's numerous chapbooks were known to have been distributed along a recognized route to Cambridge, there can be no question but that chapbooks were a familiar part of the Cambridge scene in the mid-18th century. I have carefully examined the Harding Collection of chapbooks in the Bodleian Library, Oxford, and can bear out Neuburg's generalization as regards the usual chapbook trade of stories and miscellanies of fact and superstition which passed for the people's penny encyclopaedias of their day.

Dicey's story is at once complex and fascinating. St Ives had *three* newspapers before the end of 1719, of which one, the *St Ives Postboy,* printed its last issue on 6 February 1719. Its editor, Robert Raikes, then joined forces with William Dicey, who left London after 12 April 1719. The first issue of their *St Ives Mercury* was dated 13 October 1719 and the only surviving copy has a more than passing interest for Cambridgeshire street literature in its advertisement for a chapbook. This was *"A Consolatory Epistle to the Jacks of Great Britain*. Sold at the Printing-office in St Ives [by Dicey] and to be had of W. Smith in Cambridge . . ." We therefore know that W. Smith was a Cambridge dealer in chapbooks late in 1719.

Dicey and Raikes left St Ives after 13 October 1719, and started *The Northampton Mercury* together on 2 May 1720. Chapmen used to deliver newspapers and collect advertisements as they sold their ballads and chapbooks, and W. Peachey of Cambridge was added to their list of agents on 23 January 1721. Of the ten known routes used by Dicey as a distribution network, one (used at least from early 1721 to the 1730s) was to Cambridge by way of Bedford.

Dicey's trade in Cambridge can be proved from an imprint on the chapbook *Faithful friendship or, Alphonso and Ganselo:* **'sold by William Peachey, near St. Bene't's Church, in Cambridge**, at Burnham's snuff-shop in Aylesbury; Mrs Margaret Ward, in Sun Lane, Reading, Paul Stevens in Bicester; Tho. Williams in Tring; Anthony Thorpe in St. Albans; John Timbs and Henry Potter, in Stony Stratford; and by Churrude Brady in St Ives. At all which places, chapmen, travellers, &c., may be furnished with all sorts of old and new ballads, broadsheets, histories, &c'.

William Dicey's chapbooks printed at Northampton fed the London warehouse of Dicey and Marshall which was to pass, through Dicey's son Cluer and Marshall's son John, to Joseph Pitts. And Pitts (with Jemmy Catnach) was to be instrumental in the revival of the ballad and chapbook trade in the 19th century.

As Leslie Shepard writes, "chapbooks began as a kind of printed folklore. Like broadsides they had quaint woodcut illustrations, but they had a broader scope than the ballads. Chapbooks retold old romances and fairy-tales, related stories of ancient battles, rehashed superstitions and riddles, interpreted dreams, foretold the future, exhorted sinners to repentance, or simply cracked jokes. These penny histories were the books of poor people, and coloured their outlook and philosophy".

Samuel Pepys, whose library and magnificent collection of broadside ballads passed to his old college, Magdalene, in 1724, was also a keen collector of chapbooks, binding up one volume of them with the title *Penny Godlinesses,* and three more (of 115 chapbooks) with the title *Penny Merriments.* From the first volume of *Penny Merriments* I have selected for reprinting passages from the tale of Tom Hickathrift for its Cambridgeshire connections. This chapbook was printed by J[ohn] M[illet] for William Thackeray and Thomas Passinger. William Thackeray sold his chapbooks 'at the Angel in Duck-Lane, London' and the style and subject-matter may be considered representative of the chapbooks read by Cambridge schoolchildren in the 1680s and beyond.

THE Pleasant HISTORY of *Thomas Hic-ka-thrift.*
His Birth and Parentage, and the true manner of his performing many Manly Acts, and how he killed a Gyant.
Young man, here thou mayest behold what Honour *Tom* came unto.

And if that thou dost buy this Book,
Be sure that thou dost in it look;
And read it o're, then thou wilt say,
Thy money is not thrown away.

In the Reign before William the Conqueror, I have read in ancient Histories, that there dwelt a Man in the Marsh of the Isle of Ely, in the County of Cambridge, whose Name was Thomas Hic-ka-thrift, a poor Man, and day labourer, yet he was a very stout Man, and able to perform two days works instead of one, he having one Son, and no more Children in the world, he called him by his own Name Thomas Hickathrift; this old Man put his Son to good Learning, but he would take none, for he was, as we call them now in this Age, none of the wisest sort, but something soft, and had no docity at all in him: God calling this Old Man his Father out of the world, his Mother being tender of him, and maintained him by her hand labour as well as she could: he being sloathful and not willing to work to get a penny for his living, but all his delight was to be in the Chimney corner, and would eat as much at one time as might very well serve four or five ordinary men, for he was in length when he was but Ten years of age, about eight foot, and in Thickness five foot, and his Hand was like unto a shoulder of Mutton, and in all parts from top to toe, he was like a Monster; and yet his great Strength was not known.

How *Tom Hic-ka-thrift's* Strength came to be known; the which if you please but to read, will give you full satisfaction.

THE first time that his Strength was known, was by his Mothers going to a Rich Farmers House, (she being but a poor Woman) to desire a Bottle of Straw to shift her self and her son Thomas: the Farmer being an honest Charitable Man, bid her take what she would: she going home to her Son *T*om, said, I pray thee go to such a place and fetch me a Bottle of Straw, I have asked him leave: he swore a great Oath he would not go; nay, prithee *T*om go, said his old Mother, he swore again he would not go, unless she would borrow him a Cart-rope, she being willing to please him, because she would have some Straw, went and borrowed him a Cart-rope to his desire, he taking it went his way;

so coming to the Farmers House, the Master was in the Barn, and two men a Thrashing: said *T*om, I am come for a Bottle of Straw: *T*om, said the Master, take as much as thou canst carry; he laid down his Cart-rope, and began to make his Bottle; but, said they, *T*om, thy rope is too short, and jeer'd poor Tom, but he fitted the man well for it, for he made his bottle, and when he had made it, there was supposed to be a Load of Straw in it of two thousand weight; but, said they, what a great fool art thou? thou canst not carry the Tith on't; but *T*om took the Bottle and flung it on his shoulder, and made no more of it then we do of an hundred weight, to the great admiration of Master and men. Tom Hic-ka-thrift's strength being known in the Town, then they would not let him any longer lye basking by the fire in the Chimney-corner, every one would be hiring him to work, they seeing him to have so much strength, told him that it was a shame for him to live such a lazy course of life, and to lye idle day after day as he did. So *T*om seeing them bait at him in such a manner as they did, he went first to one work, then to another, but at length came a Man to *T*om, and desired him to go with him unto the Wood, for he had a Tree to bring home, and he would content him. So *T*om went with him, and he took with him four Men beside; but when they came to the Wood, they set the Cart by the Tree and began to draw it up with Pullies, but *T*om seeing them not able to lift it up, said *S*tand away you Fools, and takes the Tree and sets it on one end, and lays it in the Cart, now says he, see what a Man can do; Marry, it is true, said they: so when they had done, coming through the Wood they met the Woodman, *T*om asked him for a stick to make his Mother a fire with; I, said the Woodman, take one what thou canst carry: so *T*om espyed a Tree bigger then was in the Cart, and lays it on his Shoulder, and goes home with it as fast as the Cart went and six Horses could draw it: This was the second time that *T*oms Strength was known: so when *T*om began to know that he had more Strength than twenty Men had, he then began to be Merry with Men, and very tractable, and would Run, or Go, or Jump; and took great delight to be amongst Company, and to go to Fairs and Meetings, and to see Sports and Pastime: So going to a Feast, the Young Men were all met, some to Cudgels, some to Wrastling, some throwing the Hammer, and the like; so *T*om stood a little to see their Sport, and at last goes to them that were a throwing the Hammer, and standing a little by to behold their Man-like Sport, as last he takes the Hammer in his hand, to feel the weight of it, and bid them stand out of the way, for he would throw it as far as he could: I, said the Smith, and jeer'd poor Tom, you'l throw it a great way i'le warrant you: but *T*om took the Hammer and flung it, and there was a River about five or six Furlungs off, and flung it into that: so when he had done he bid the Smith go fetch his Hammer again, and laught the Smith to scorn; but when *T*om had done that, he would go to Wrastling, though he had no more skill than an Ass had, but what he did by Strength, yet he flung all that came, for if once he laid hold they were gone: some he would throw over his head, some he would lay down slyly and how he pleased: he would not lock nor strike at their Heels, but flung them two or three Yards from him, ready to break their Necks asunder: so that none at last durst go into the Ring to wrastle with him, for they took him to be some Devil that was come amongst them, so *T*om's fame was spread more in the Country.

The *Hickathrift* format is 14 x 8½ cm: the chapbook consists of 24 pages altogether, of which 4 are preliminaries, 18 are text pages, and the two final leaves bear woodcut illustrations.

The foregoing takes up pp.3-6 of the chapbook; pp.7-13 tell 'How *Tom* came to be a Brewers Man, and how he cam to kill a Gyant, and at last was Mr. *Hic-ka-thrift*'; 'How *Tom* kept a pack of Hounds, and kickt a Foot-ball quite away; and how he had like to have been Robbed by four Thieves, and how he escaped' takes up pp.14-18; p.19 shows a woodcut of a rustic with a stave, while p.20 depicts in cuts the several feats of Tom Hickathrift.

Now that Huntingdon falls into Cambridgeshire, following the local government reorganization of 1974, my Taylor and Burton execution tract has added interest for the students of Cambridgeshire street literature. Printed by A. Applegath and E. Cowper, Nelson-Place, Gravel-Lane, Southwark, and priced 'one penny', it is entitled *Narrow Escape from the Punishment of Death; or, The Case of John Taylor and John Burton who were left for execution at Huntingdon,* and can be dated by internal evidence to the second decade of the 19th century. My copy measures 17½ x 10 cm, but it has been trimmed into the text. The six-page story is followed by a two-page hymn.

The narrator explains how he managed to obtain a reprieve for the two men, convicted of sheep-stealing and due to be executed. "Soon after I had quitted the prison, and had reached my inn, I saw the people flocking in all directions [for the execution]. A friend of mine soon called, and suggested that it might be advisable for me not to be seen in the town, as the mob many of whom, had come from distant parts of the county, were not pleased at their disappointment. The pity which I felt for these poor men, and the horror at the want of feeling shewn by the crowd, have made an impression upon me which no time can efface'. The events recorded took place in 1801.

A 'garland' is defined by the 19th-century bookseller John Camden Hotten, in his MS. 'The Popular Literature of the Olden Time; Merry and Serious' (Bodleian Library, Harding Collection), as a 'popular name for . . . little collections of perhaps half a dozen songs with a showy woodcut on the title'. Hotten, writing about 1870, cites a typical chapbook of about 1755 (his p.147) entitled *The Cambridge Jests or, Wit's Recreations*, and consisting of 24 pages. 'The amount of fun contained in these chapbooks', writes Hotten, 'appeared inexhaustible, and a singular motley must John Chapman's wallet have presented when at some little roadside Inn – long before shilling sentimental novels in glaring paperhanging covers flooded the country – he was prevailed upon to open and exhibit his treasures. In the words of the title of one of these humorous little productions he would, no doubt, address his gaping audience in this style. "Nimble and Quick, Pick and Chuse where you will. Here is something to fit and please everybody, containing the humours of the age, being whimsical, witty, diverting, and comical with useful remarks on the virtues and vices of the times" '.

John Camden Hotten (p.180) quotes the following from *The Cambridge Jests:*

'A Merry and witty Cambridge scholar going from London to Colchester in a cold wet day, and coming to an inn, gave the hostler his horse, and immediately went into the kitchen to warm himself, but an unmannerly company of the townsmen surrounded the fire, so that the parson could not come near, whereupon he bid the ostler give his horse a peck of oysters. – Will your horse eat them, said he? Pray try, said the other. So the townsmen hearing this, left the fire to see the wonder, and in the interim the parson took the best seat by the fire. The ostler having made trial, brought back the oysters, saying, the horse would not touch them. Well, said the other, if he will not, I'll try if I can. The men perceiving the plot, leering at one another

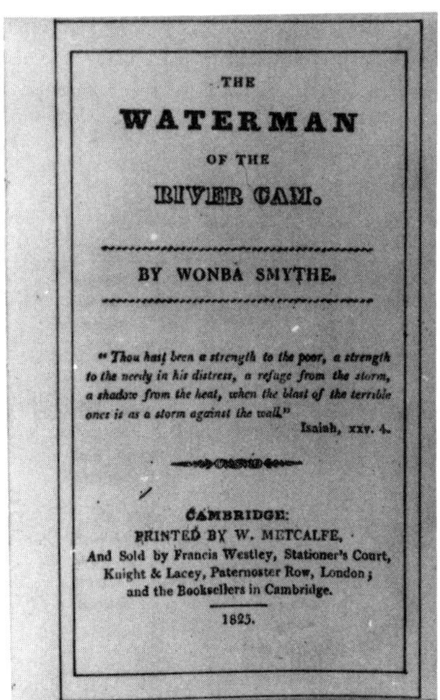

THE
WATERMAN
OF THE
RIVER CAM.

BY WONBA SMYTHE.

"Thou hast been a strength to the poor, a strength to the needy in his distress, a refuge from the storm, a shadow from the heat, when the blast of the terrible ones is as a storm against the wall."

Isaiah, xxv. 4.

CAMBRIDGE:
PRINTED BY W. METCALFE,
And Sold by Francis Westley, Stationer's Court,
Knight & Lacey, Paternoster Row, London;
and the Booksellers in Cambridge.

1825.

THE WATERMAN OF THE RIVER CAM
Religious tract in chapbook style printed by Metcalfe in Cambridge, 1825. Title-page 13 x 8 cm. (*Cambridgeshire Collection*)

laughed, but were ashamed to tarry.

Like the chapbooks which reached Cambridge from London and Northampton, religious tracts were by and large not printed in Cambridge. The *Cambridge Chronicle* of 27 August 1808 (p.3) advertizes the Religious Tract Depository, Market Street, Cambridge. 'E. Wright, Agent for the Cambridgeshire Society for Promoting Religious Knowledge, respectfully informs the Members of that Society and the public in general, that he has on sale a large assortment of Religious Tracts at the London prices'. Religious societies of this kind commonly distributed tracts to the poor, who might then sell them very cheaply, earning for themselves whatever they might be given; many such tract-sellers were, or pretended to be, wounded veterans of the army or navy.

The Waterman of the River Cam is more of a religious tract than a chapbook in the traditional sense of the word, and its late date (1825) conforms to the period of the rise of the solemn tract. But it possesses the distinction of being, so far as is known, the only tract in the chapbook style printed in Cambridge, and as a curiosity it was reprinted photographically (with a new front cover) in 1972 by the now defunct Cokaygne Press, Cambridge. This reprint has become (such is the irony in collecting printed ephemera) almost as scarce as the original.

Collections of religious tracts can be found in the British Library; Cambridge University Library; Bodleian Library, Oxford; Methodist Archives; and in the S.P.C.K. Archives, S.P.C.K. House, London.

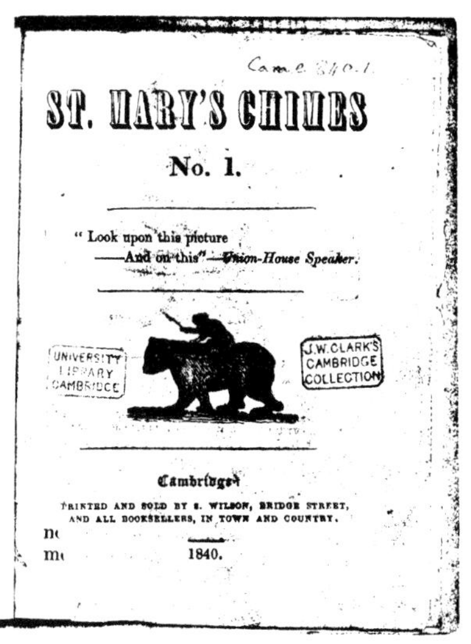

ST. MARY'S CHIMES

No. 1.

" Look upon this picture
—And on this"—Union-House Speaker.

Cambridge:

PRINTED AND SOLD BY S. WILSON, BRIDGE STREET, AND ALL BOOKSELLERS, IN TOWN AND COUNTRY.

1840.

ST. MARY'S CHIMES. A chapbook printed by S. Wilson of Bridge Street, Cambridge, in 1840, and using some of the old cuts from broadside ballads. No. 1 (all known). 13 x 9 cm. (*Cambridge University Library, Clark Collection*)

Further Reading

Chapbooks

Ashton, John. *Chap-books of the eighteenth century.* New York, 1967. [Following the original London edition of 1882.]

Gomme, G.L. *and* Wheatley, H.B. *Chapbooks and folk-lore tracts.* 5 vols. London, 1885.

Halliwell-Phillips, James O. *A catalogue of chap-books, garlands, and popular histories.* London, 1849.

Neuburg, Victor E. *Chapbooks: a guide to reference material on English, Scottish and American chapbook literature of the eighteenth and nineteenth centuries.* London, 1964. 2nd. ed., 1972.

Neuburg, Victor E. 'The Diceys and the chapbook trade'. In *The Library*, 5th ser., vol. XXIV, no. 3, 1969.

Neuburg, Victor E. *The penny histories: a study of chapbooks for young readers over two centuries.* London, 1968.

Thompson, Roger. *ed. Samuel Pepys' 'Penny Merriments'.* London, 1976. [A selection from the 3 vols. of chapbooks of the cited title in the Pepysian Library, Magdalene College, Cambridge.]

Weiss, Harry B. *A book about chapbooks.* Trenton, N.J., 1942. [Originally issued in only 100 copies, the first edition has now been reproduced in facsimile.]

Religious Tracts

Hewitt, Gordon. *Let the people read.* London, 1949. [On the Religious Tract Society.]

Spinney, G.H. 'Cheap Repository Tracts: Hazard and Marshall Edition'. In *The Library,* 4th ser., vol. XX, 1939.

Spurgeon, C.H. *and others. Booksellers and bookbuyers in byeways and highways.* London, 1882. [The purpose and methods of tract distribution in 19th-century England.]

Posters and Handbills

A 'poster' may be defined as a printed public notice of sufficiently large dimensions to be read on a wall from the other side of the road, whereas the term 'handbill' is used here to denote a printed public notice (often also reproduced by methods other than traditional letterpress, including duplicating, but not including handwritten, unique messages such as graffiti), designed chiefly to be distributed through the letterbox.

The study of public notices has two main uses. Firstly, it enables the social historian to collect data on the principal concerns and preoccupations of local government, local societies, pressure groups and individuals who seek to impose their policies and attitudes on the world at large. Secondly, it enables the printing historian to collect examples of the kind of type faces and styles dominant in each period of jobbing printing, which may be significantly different from the examples he knows from book printing of the same period. Thus, in *Cambridge revisited* (1921; 2nd ed., 1974), Arthur B. Gray chooses to typify life in Cambridge not so much by conventional topographical scenes (though those are present too), but rather by an advertisement printed by Francis Hodson for William Gallyon, a gunmaker of Green Street; and by a coaching timetable printed by Samuel Wilson in 1834 for William Ekin & Co., operating the Leicester stagecoach from the Hoop Hotel.

The Cambridgeshire Collection (Central Library) offers the most comprehensive archive of Cambridge posters and handbills, one of the earliest being the warning of an escaped lunatic of 1790.

Coulson's, the Cambridge printers, have kindly given a wide selection of their printed ephemera to the Cambridgeshire Collection, and one would like to see more printers negotiating agreements with Local Studies Collections in public and county library systems for the systematic retention of ephemera they issue, no matter how apparently slight. It is after all as utterly misleading to view the history of printing as a series of masterpieces by the Baskervilles, Plantins, and Bodonis or their like, as it is to study world literature only through its masterpieces. If the historian realizes that Marie Corelli sold more copies of her books than any other writer in England since Shakespeare, it must at least interest him to see what kind of writer she was, even if his eventual judgment on her work is harsh. Thus with the hundreds of thousands of handbills that are written, set up in a particular typeface, on a particular paper, to serve the immediate needs or purposes of men. If we ignore these messages we ignore the greater mass of mankind.

The Cambridge and County Folk Museum possesses a relatively small collection of printed ephemera, but much of the material is of absorbing

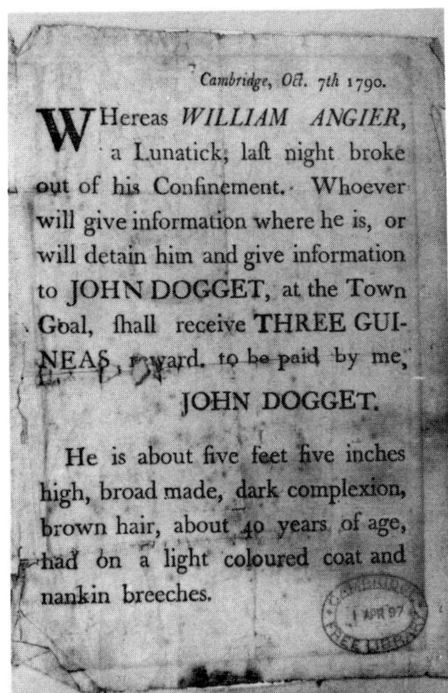

Cambridge, Oct. 7th 1790.

WHereas *WILLIAM ANGIER*, a Lunatick, laſt night broke out of his Confinement. Whoever will give information where he is, or will detain him and give information to JOHN DOGGET, at the Town Goal, ſhall receive THREE GUINEAS, reward, to be paid by me,

JOHN DOGGET.

He is about five feet five inches high, broad made, dark complexion, brown hair, about 40 years of age, had on a light coloured coat and nankin breeches.

WHereas WILLIAM ANGIER, a Lunatick . . . Public notice on an escaped lunatic printed in Cambridge, 1790. 24 x 18 cm. (*Cambridgeshire Collection*)

ENGLISH MASTIFFS.

WE, by this Addreſs, publicly and ſolemnly, before God and our Country, pledge our Fortunes, Perſons, and Lives in the Defence of our Sovereign and all the Bleſſings of our glorious Conſtitution.

There is not a Man who hears me, I am perſuaded, who is not prompt and eager to redeem that pledge. There is not, there cannot be a Man here, who would leave undefended our good, tried, and brave *OLD KING* in the Hour of Danger.

No, Sir! we need now no Warning-voice; no ſtring of Eloquence; no Thoughts that heat, and Words that burn, are neceſſary to raiſe a Hoſt of hardy Men, when the King, the Parliament, and the Country are in Diſtreſs. CALL OUT TO YORKSHIREMEN, "*COME FORTH TO BATTLE!*"—our anſwer will be, One and All—" WE ARE READY !—*There is the Enemy! —Lead on!*"—Sir, that Enemy is not far off; a very numerous, well-appointed, ably-commanded Army, to whom is promiſed the Plunder of England, are now hovering round, and part of them in daily Sight of the promiſed Land. They view it, like as many famiſhed Wolves, Cruel as Death, and Hungry as the Grave, panting for an opportunity, at any riſk, to come into our Sheep-Fold;—*but*, and if they ſhould, is it not our Buſineſs, our firſt Duty, to have ſuch a Guard of old faithful ENGLISH MASTIFFS, of the old Breed, as ſhall make them quickly repent their temerity.

The CHIEF CONSUL of France tells us, that we are but a Nation of Shopkeepers: let us, Shopkeepers, then melt our Weights and our Scales, and return him the compliment in Bullets. Sir, we may have a firm Reliance on the Exertions of as gallant a Fleet as ever failed; but the Fleet cannot perform Impoſſibilities; it cannot be at two Places at once; it cannot conquer the Winds and ſubdue the Storms. Though our bold TARS can do much, they cannot do every thing; and it would be unſafe and daſtardly to lie ſkulking behind them. With the Bleſſing of GOD, and a good Cauſe, we can do Wonders; but, if we depend upon our Naval Proweſs only, we have much to fear. NO, Sir; ENGLAND will never be perfectly ſafe, until ſhe can Defend Herſelf as well by *Land* as by *Sea*; until ſhe can defy the haughty Foe: If there was *even a Bridge* between CALAIS and DOVER, and that Bridge in Poſſeſſion of the Enemy, ſtill ſhe can ſay, in the Language of a good *Engliſh Boxing Match*, "A FAIR FIELD AND NO FAVOUR!"

PRINTED BY F. HODSON, CAMBRIDGE.

ENGLISH MASTIFFS. An anti-Napoleon poster intended for Yorkshire but printed in Cambridge by F. Hodson in 1803. A splendid example of bellicose rhetoric fully deserving a place in any collection of Cambridge-printed street literature. 38 x 25 cm. (*Cambridge and County Folk Museum*)

interest, in particular the posters attacking Napoleon printed in 1803, when there was a distinct threat of invasion from France. Though the posters were of nationwide appeal, they were printed by F. Hodson in Cambridge, and are written with a good deal of subtlety to inflame the military ardour of the lower classes. 'WHAT A Day Labourer has to Lose IF THE French Conquer England' is the heading of one, which in the course of its eloquence asserts that 'Buonaparte has promised the plunder of all this country to his army, if they can conquer it'. 'TO ARMS! TO ARMS! Britons Strike Home!' begins another poster; a third, dated 11 August 1803, is 'A *DIALOGUE* BETWEEN Squire Worthy and his Labourer'; a fourth bays out 'ENGLISH MASTIFFS!'; while a fifth is 'Plain Answers to Plain Questions, IN A DIALOGUE BETWEEN JOHN BULL AND Bonaparte Met *Half-Seas over* between DOVER and CALAIS'.

The earliest handbills extant in the Cambridgeshire Collection which bear an imprint are those of Weston Hatfield and W. Metcalfe (Trumpington Street)

Protestants

AWAKE! AROUSE!

YOU have only one REMEDY—be united—be instant in the use of it. Petition that the Duke of Wellington, the Right Hon. Robert Peel, the Lord Chancellor, and Solicitor-General be impeached.

The Measure of Roman Catholic Emancipation they are forcing upon the Country is unconstitutional, while they are also using unconstitutional means to carry it. It is a "breaking in upon the Constitution of 1688," as they have daringly asserted. It is also an encouragement to Rebellion—will lead to a Civil War—will bring us under Foreign domination—will cause a violation of the Coronation Oath—will destroy His Majesty's best if not only Title to the Throne—will make the friends of the Government its enemies, while it will not make its enemies its friends.—Is what Parliament has no right to accede—Is in utter contempt of your Petitions and against your expressed voice. While by it they are forcing both Lords and Commons, and His Majesty also. For before the Duke of Wellington took up the measure the majority for it in the House of Commons was, I believe, never more than seven; whereas now the excess of the majority exceeds the minority, and has been 188. In the House of Lords before the same, there was always a large majority against it, and his Majesty was always and still is adverse to it. There is reason to suspect too, that they have been in communication with the Pope, contrary to the law of the land.

With all this will you suffer the measure to be carried? Will you suffer one man to govern the Kingdom, and force the whole Nation and trample upon your Laws, your Liberties, your Constitution?

Protestants! Englishmen!

AROUSE!

Consider the blood and treasure the Constitution cost your Ancestors—come forward boldly and defend it, and for this purpose, manfully and fearfully impeach the individual who would deprive you of it, and who now is most ungenerously using the honours and emoluments and confidence of a grateful country, to bring it into subjection to a Tyrant infinitely more baneful than Bonaparte ever was, and more blasting to the interests and prosperity of the Nation and of the World.—Shall he succeed?—By no means.—Arouse then! and petition for his impeachment, and that of his colleagues.—Do not despair.—Your case is not desperate—only be firm—be united—be instant.— Such is the best human means to save yourselves, while I especially urge you to prayer to Him in whose hands are the hearts and hands of all men.

I am, &c. Yours,

F. H. MABERLY

Kingston, near Caxton, Cambridgeshire,
2d April, 1829.

TALBOT & LADDS, PRINTERS, SUSSEX STREET, CAMBRIDGE.

Protestants AWAKE! AROUSE! Anti-Roman Catholic poster issued by F.H. Maberly in 1829, and printed by Talbot & Ladds of Cambridge. 37 x 24 cm. (*Cambridgeshire Collection*) in the 1820s. A Hatfield handbill of 1827 concerns the master tailors' early trade union troubles; then there is an inflammatory Maberly anti-Roman Catholic poster printed by Talbot & Ladds in 1829.

Another interesting poster against Roman Catholics, 'The Jesuits and the Popedom in Crusade against England and her faith', was printed by Metcalfe and Palmer in November 1841, and can be seen in the Folk Museum. Other printers of the 1830s and 1840s who carried out jobbing printing were Francis Hodson, C.E. Brown, Samuel Wilson, Warwick & Co., J. Hall and Henry Smith, all represented in the Cambridgeshire Collection.

The only remaining bound volume of J.W. Clark's 'Cam Papers' in the University Library (shelf-mark CUL Cam a.500.9) is entitled *Squibs and crackers* and consists of ephemera such as burlesque poems and other Varsity humour, including parodic speeches. An anonymous leaflet, *Thoughts suggested by the New Caius Gown* printed by J. Hall in 1837, provoked an immediate *Answer* . . .; and indeed the essence of these transient mementoes of university life is their power to draw quick retorts before the issue stales. An excited controversy raged in 1838 on the question of beards and moustaches worn by Cambridge undergraduates. The burlesque *Rape of the Whisker: an heroic poem* was published by W.P. Grant in 1838 and reached a second edition in the same year. Another such, *Fuzwhiskiana,* was printed by Metcalfe & Palmer for W.P. Grant in 1838.

One of the joys of the John Johnson Collection in the Bodleian Library is the mass of material on Cambridge elections. Until recently it was necessary to study the history of elections by the use of contemporary newspapers and such primary sources as election addresses or satirical squibs in the form of handbills, pamphlets, or wall posters. In the pamphlet boxes 'Elections' for example, there is a series beginning *Election Flights. Containing, The Nomination Day, a letter from Timmy Straightforward to his Mother, and a new song,* a street pamphlet of 32 pp. favouring Granby and dated on page [5] May 23 1780. The imprint read 'London printed: sold by J. Almon, Piccadilly; W. Cowper, Cambridge; and all other booksellers'. The price of this first skit was not printed, but *A second letter from Timmy Straightforward to his Mother. Containing a description of Pot-Fair, and an Ode for the Anniversary Meeting of the Governors of Addenbrooke's Hospital, Cambridge,* bearing the same imprint, was 12 pp. long and priced at sixpence. This was followed by *A third letter* (12 pp.) and *A fourth letter . . . To which is prefixed, an address to Anti-Straightforward* (15 pp.), indicating that the opposition had already become vocal. Two such anti-Timmy squibs are also found in the Bodleian: *An address to Timmy Straighforward. By a friend*, 11 pp. long, dated 1781, with the London imprint changed to Almon and Debret; and *A Letter from Mrs. Straightforward to her Son Timmy,* 15 pp. long, priced at one shilling but undated, and with the Cambridge imprint of J. Deighton only.

Absentee M.P.s were a constant source of irritation to their supporters and of glee to their opponents. The Whigs thus attacked the Tory Lord C.S.

Manners, Duke of Rutland: 'Missing. IF THE GENTLEMAN who has lately absented himself from Cambridgeshire should see this, he is most earnestly requested to return , or to furnish some clue by means of which A LINE may be sent to him' (undated but printed by W. Metcalfe, All Saints' Passage, Cambridge; in the Bodleian). The Whigs, proposing Pryme and Spring-Rice for Parliament, had an anti-Sugden poster printed by Metcalfe on November 20 1832 to read 'Sudden Visitation! A WHITE Ghost in BARNWELL' (also in the Bodleian), ridiculing the long absences of the Tory Sir Edward Sugden.

To study election posters and handbills in Cambridge, it is necessary to go to the University Library and the Cambridgeshire Collection, which are strongest on mid-19th century elections. Two posters of 1834 – one for the Tories and another for the Whigs – indicate the virulence with which campaigning was tainted.

In 1831, the Whig printer Samuel Wilson issued *Squibiana: a collection of addresses, songs, & other effusions, published during the late Election*, edited by one 'Mat Wildfire'. Wilson had printed many of these squibs himself. A scurrilous attack on Cambridge voters, for instance, dated 11 August 1830, opened its support of the Whigs Osborne and Adeane as follows: "AN ODE FOR ASSES, appointed to be sung or said in celebration of the EIGHTH RETURN of Lord C.S. Manners to Parliament, as the Non Representative of the County of Cambridge".

Joshua King, President of Queens' College and Vice-Chancellor of the University, allegedly demanded that all his staff and dependents entitled to vote in the 1834 General Election should vote for the Tory candidate, Sugden. The Whigs retaliated with a number of squibs, including the celebrated 'Bribery, Coercion, Corruption and Intimidation', probably by Professor J.S. Henslow, which left nobody in doubt as to the charges. A gardener at Queens', one James King, nevertheless defied the President, saying that he intended to vote for Spring-Rice, and was dismissed accordingly. A long letter was issued by the Tories attacking Henslow, and the most durable street sign ever known in Cambridge (HENSLOW COMMON INFORMER) could be made out on a wall of Corpus Christi until 1895 and beyond.

The general tenor of raucous satire which characterized Cambridge political squibs of this period can be studied in Tory posters such as *UNRIVALLED!!!* or *CIRCUS.* (illustrated here) printed by J. Hall. The latter is not, as one might imagine at first sight, anything so simple as an advertisement for a travelling circus. Its performers (animal and otherwise) are the Cambridge Whigs of the time. 'Nslow' is of course Henslow and 'Springo Roder-rico' is Spring-Rice. The 'Knight of the Poker' is Henry Gunning, Esquire Bedell from 1789 until his death in 1854. 'Primo' is the Whig M.P. Professor Pryme and 'Juliano' is Julian Skrine. 'Jim Crow' is Thomas Milner Gibson, and 'Wado' is Edward Wade of Petty Cury. The 'Rival Clowns' are so called because both Samuel Wilson ('Samivel Vilsun') and Weston Hatfield were in the printing business; their work is illustrated in the present study.

The Whigs replied to *CIRCUS* with their own *THE TORY CONJUROR!*

Mr. KING,

PRESIDENT OF QUEENS COLLEGE,

Vice-Chancellor,

AND

JAMES KING,

HIS GARDENER.

The STATEMENT of JAMES KING, as made by him in Mr. SPRING RICE's COMMITTEE-ROOM:—

Committee.—Mr. JAMES KING, are you Gardener to Mr. King the President of Queen's College and the present Vice-Chancellor of the University?

Answer.—I am.

Committee.—Are you a Ten-pound Householder?

Answer.—I am.

Committee.—Has any thing passed between the Vice-Chancellor and yourself concerning this election?

Answer.—Yes.

Committee.—Have the goodness to state what has passed?

Answer.—The Vice-Chancellor sent John Massey his Butler, to me several times. I believe the first time was on Thursday last. I wont be positive as to the day. The first time, he came with *the Vice-Chancellor's compliments*, if I had not promised my vote to Mr. Rice, he wished me to promise it for Sir Edward Sugden. I stated in answer, that I did not intend to vote for Sir Edward, and that I would not make a promise to either party. The Butler was sent to me again, requesting that I would promise not to vote for Mr. Rice. I then requested him to give my duty to the Vice-Chancellor, and that I was extremely sorry to act in opposition to him; but that I could not make that promise. This same message was repeated several times—three at the least. On Saturday morning I received intimation that the Vice-Chancellor wanted to speak to me. I went in the evening when I went to the Lodge, between Seven and Eight,—I dare say it was Eight—to speak to him. He asked me to go into the Dining Room with him. When we were there, he said, he wished to know, whether I had decided about making any promise as to my vote. I said, I was very sorry to act in opposition to him—that I could not vote for Sir Edward, and I could not make a promise not to vote for Mr. Rice. He said, he felt very strongly upon the question; and, in consequence of my objecting to make that promise, he said, HE WAS DETERMINED NOT TO KEEP A MAN UPON THE PREMISES WHO DIFFERED FROM HIM; and that he wished me to understand such was his determination. I said, I was exceedingly sorry it should happen so; but, I wished as he was determined I should leave, that he would fix a time for me to leave. To this he made no answer.

Committee.—Mr. King and you have been upon good terms?

Answer.—Yes, the best; no Master could behave kinder than he has done.

Committee.—Your conduct does you infinite honor; both in the kindness with which you speak of your master, and in the moral courage which you have shown on this occasion. The town is under great obligations to you

Answer.—I would do any thing else to oblige him. He is beloved by Fellows, Students and Servants. But I felt this to be a public duty, between God and my conscience.

(Signed) JAMES KING.

PEOPLE OF CAMBRIDGE!—The above transaction openly avows the meaning of the *Vice-Chancellor's Compliments*, which the University Marshal and the President's Butler have been carrying round the town, during the last week. Electors! will you submit to this? You had better be robbed of your Votes by an Overseer, and be turned back again into a Corporation Borough, than be eternally disgraced by voting against your consciences, through base submission to such unjustifiable interference. Be firm and honest. Your enemies threaten you with what, as public officers, they dare not do. Do you but your duty now, and as private men, when the Election is over, they will respect you more than if, by being traitors to your opinions, you publish yourselves their slaves. Follow the example set you by an honest man, and you can run no danger from which you shall not be protected by your friends.

***June 9th*, 1834.**

W. HATFIELD, PRINTER, CAMBRIDGE.

Mr. KING, PRESIDENT OF QUEENS COLLEGE. Political poster issued by the Whigs on behalf of Thomas Spring-Rice to discredit the Tories for alleged corruption, printed in Cambridge by Weston Hatfield, 1834. 44½ x 28 cm. (*Cambridgeshire Collection*)

CIRCUS.

Positively the Last Night!

The Manager of the Circus begs to inform the Liberals of Cambridge and its vicinity, that (in consequence of the [illegible] support which he has received from that body) he has entered into an engagement with several well-known Reformers and *Impostors* [illegible], with a view to give the Inhabitants a plentiful and rich fund of amusement during the ensuing week; Wednesday being positively the last night.

The performance will commence with an entire new scene, entitled

Make way for Liberty!!!

Showing the various and delusive ways used by the falsely-termed Liberals (assisted by their famous Bog Trotter from the Sister Country) to deceive and cajole the Electors of Cambridge, and to "astonish the Natives."

Knight of the Poker ... ... *An Old Stager.* [illegible] ... ... *A Nobody-knows what.*
Springe-Rodee-rico ... ... *A Bog Trotter with a slight touch of the brogue.*
[illegible] ... ... *Cad to Springe-Rodee-rico.* [illegible] ... ... *A man of great INFORMATION.*
Bullies, Irishmen, &c. &c.

After which (by particular desire) will be presented, the

Cantabrigian Statues,

Representing beautiful imitations of Modern Characters.

This arrangement is made in order to convey to the political taste of the Electors, in an effective manner, a series of these remarkable characters, the fidelity of which will be recognized by every one, as they are bodied from descriptions by the very best authorities.—The following is the order of the Portraits:—

1st.—*The Beggarman* in four well-known attitudes.
2nd.—*The Thimble Rigger* in three attitudes.
3rd.—*Rice* at Limeric defying the Electors of Cambridge.
4th.—*The Whig, Rice the* **M. P.** grinding his teeth whilst overhearing the Poor Man's invective against the Union.
5th.—*The Whigs* alarmed at the *Tories.* (This representation will conclude with three celebrated positions of the rejected Candidates.)

After which (for the first time here) will be introduced, a

MASQUERADE and CARNIVAL.

Wherein Mr. R. will introduce himself in a variety of Different Characters, commencing with the Punchinello of the Irishmen, the Whigs "*prime*" votary, whose chant is the contralto of discordance, and whose vagaries are particularly [illegible], by throwing his limbs into all imaginable contortion and dislocation: if the Spectators will admit of the momentary supposition that Mr. R. in this character is the original person, they will be better able to judge of the qualities of the Performer; he will then change with amazing rapidity into the *Buffo of the House of Commons*; again, he will appear in a most insinuating character, *smoothed over* with a little blarney.—But to enumerate all the various opposite characters which he assumes, would far exceed the limits of a hand-bill.

BY THE COMPANY.

THE CINDER-DIRT MAN,
DOCTOR GINN, *a Travelling Encyclopædia,*
CINDER-DIRT Jun., *a chip of the Old Block,*
HYDROPHOBIANNA, *a Literary Gent.*
HUMPHREY CLINKER,
TIMOTHY CUNNING, *a dealer in Old Pots.*

To be followed (the only time here) by an entire NEW ACT, entitled

Jim Crow

And His Tiger.

In which MR. ROGER will introduce several feats of ECONOMY, also showing his opinions of Reform and Revolution; by particular request he will introduce

A GROTESQUE LITTLE ANIMAL called

WADO!

Or the Petty-Cury MONKEY.

Exhibiting the amazing Tricks, Feats, and agility of that

SINGULAR LITTLE ANIMAL;

Rival Clowns, Messrs. SAMIVEL VILSUN and WESTON.

The whole to conclude with the laughable Farce of

SIMPSON and Co.

Or How to get a VOTE.

Characters by the Company.

LITTLE BILLY SNIP. MASTER BASHFUL. THE PERSECUTED CLERK. SERGEANT BLACK HORSE.
Officers, Servants, &c.

The Managers beg leave to return their grateful thanks for the support which they have hitherto met with, and would wish for a continuance of favours.

N. B.—*Persons are requested to send in their bills before 12 o'Clock on Wednesday, as the Manager will leave the Place early on Thursday Morning.*

J. HALL, PRINTER, OPPOSITE THE PITT PRESS.

Wonderful Deceptions! printed by Wilson.

While a number of printers were committed to one faction (Naylor for the Tories, for instance, or Wilson for the Whigs), there are cases of printers who placed their machinery at the disposal of either party, as most printers would do nowadays. Thus, J. Hall printed a scurrilous cartoon captioned MANNERS HAS RESIGNED!!! which offends the English sense of fair play by kicking a man when he is down. The Tory M.P. is shown vomiting, the legend alleging that he was 'seized with a severe vomiting, and actually died 10 minutes after his safe arrival [at Westminster]. Rumour says that he had partaken so largely of corruption that he expired without a struggle! . . .' But the Cambridgeshire Collection also possess squibs and posters for the Tories Sir A.C. Grant and Hon. H.M. Sutton. Grant, who owned slaves in Jamaica, was twice elected in Cambridge, but resigned with a letter printed by the Tory printer C.E. Brown on 13 March 1843, when the Tory candidate Fitzroy Kelly offered himself as a replacement. Glover and Foister of Falcon Yard, Petty Cury, normally printed for the Whigs, as did Weston Hatfield. Hodson & Brown printed for C.P. Yorke the Tory, beaten when opposing the Reform candidate John Walbanke Childers in the 1832 election. The Whig W. Metcalfe printed for Childers.

In a printed broadside 'Straining at a Knat and swallowing a Camel' (undated but *c.* 1846), the indignant Wilson attacked the publication 'Purity and Impartiality' to show that the Conservative-dominated city corporation had awarded contracts for official printing jobs almost exclusively to Tory printers:

1840-45

Treasurer's books	£	s	d
TALBOT (Tory) was given by the Corporation printing work worth	227	7	8
Metcalfe & Palmer (Whigs or neutral)	95	9	6
Hall (Tory)	53	13	3
Foister (Tory)	47	14	0
Warwick & Co. (Whig)	27	5	6
Wilson (Whig)	5	18	0

In 1846 the contracts were shared principally between Talbot and Foister, both Conservatives.

Cambridge printers were never averse to attacking each other openly. Thus, Henry Smith of Market Hill, printer of the Whig *Cambridge Independent Press* attacks another printer, Charles Edward Brown, in the handbill *Electors of West Barnwell* in reply to a pro-Tory handbill issued by Brown on the same day, 15 December 1843. Brown had on 16 May 1840 printed the bill 'To the Worthy and Independent Electors of the East and West Barnwell Wards'

◁ **CIRCUS.** Political poster printed on behalf of the Tories by J. Hall of Cambridge. *c.* 1834. 57 x 22½ cm. (*Cambridgeshire Collection*)

CAUTION !!!

To ROBERT BARNARD, the man who sold his Wife, and who, in conjunction with one who throws over his shoulders a black gown, as a cloak, to screen his dark and hideous form and corrupt deeds in iniquity, with a cloven foot, requires only the harpoon tail to fashion him out completely in the disguise of the Devil. A Pettifogger of so low a grade is not to be met even in the precincts of St. Giles, the fellow Barnard calls this detestable Miscreant his legal adviser. I say fearlessly at once his legal Robber and ill adviser, look at the Scorpion's Caution, placarded throughout Cambridge, a stink and disgrace to the very walls they are stuck on. Again the vile Slanderer has the audacity of accusing me of Adultery. Away with such reptiles and calumniators, I dare him or any of his conspirators to prove that infamous charge against me. I call upon the Villain to make good the assertion by boldly coming forward and instituting proceedings against the Adulterer. Happy and proud shall I be to meet the charge, knowing it to be false. I defy the scoundrel, or any other person or persons, to prove a single fact against me of inconstancy. I treat such base insinuation with that contempt it justly merits (altho' be it known, the Villain sold me,) whether for dissection or not I cannot tell, but I am still in the land of the living, and the laws of my Country, thank Heaven, protect me, and are a strong and true shield against the poisoned arrows continually aimed at me for destruction. In answer to the Rascal's caution, I beg to state he has no property or power whatever in or upon Grafton House, and Premises at Newmarket, nor has he there any Tenant or Servants, (which will soon be made known, as the said Grafton House and Premises will be immediately offered for Public Sale by Auction, and will positively be sold without reserve, with a good and sufficient title to the purchaser of the Estate, (be whom he may). These are facts the said robert Barnard is too well aware off to require further comment.

I am sorry to add a more debauched character than this very Robert Barnard, is not in existence, or in the annals of History. —Look at a case which took place in Petty cury, Cambridge, where a Father who professes religion, and who actually assisted in his Child's ruin and destruction by fetching boot-jack, slippers and a lighted candle, and leading the said Robert Barnard to the bed-room of his own daughter, in which bed Barnard slept with the daughter, I ask is not this horrible and disgusting to the ear of parents? Many times has he left my bed for the purpose of visiting this girl whose little finger, he said, he liked better than my body, and many other females whose names I decline to mention, fearful of the injury it might do them in the exposure; (the truth will soon be known as respects the things between us.) A Court of Justice will set matters right in a very short period, when the Public will be put in possession of the real merits of the case. Robert Barnard must not expect any support from me in future, he will find out when too late his disgraceful treatment to an inoffensive and injured woman and deeply regret the many times he has told me to go into the Streets and get my living, I vow and declare the Villain Robert Barnard, nor any of his treacherous friends, shall ever again receive one farthing from the falsely accused, and basely abused

Cambridge, July 12, 1841. MARTHA BARNARD.

CAUTION!!! Wall poster printed anonymously for Martha Barnard in 1841 to rebut a wall poster by Robert Barnard, presumably couched in similar terms, entitled 'The Scorpion's Caution'. 43 x 28½ cm. (*Cambridgeshire Collection*)

(signed by one 'Hezekiah Grubbins') against the Whig denunciation of bribery which led to the loss of the Tory Sutton's seat. Other Tory posters of the time included J. Hall's 'Dogs in a Manger!!' and 'Unparalleled Lies of the Whigs' and C.E. Brown's 'Electors of Cambridge', dated 4 May 1840 and ridiculing Foster's accusation that Samuel Lang bribed George Smith with 9 sovereigns to vote for Mr Manners Sutton.

Political scandals of the 1850s form an important part of Cambridge street literature. Kenneth Macaulay and John Harvey Astell were elected from Cambridge in 1853, but due to allegations of bribery their election was declared void on 1 March. The Cambridgeshire Collection has a malicious parody by an unnamed Whig printer (Wilson?) allegedly emanating from 'Nail 'em & Co.', Printers, "Lying and Bribery Office", Cambridge, to attack Naylor & Co. of the *Cambridge Chronicle* Office. It is headed "CALENDAR of the Criminal Bribers, Scoundrels, and Corruptors, who will take their Trials before the Hon. Graham Willmore, George Bowden and Thomas Towher, Esquires, Her Majesty's Royal Commissioners, on Tuesday next, June the 7th 1853, and following days, at the Town Hall, in the Borough of Cambridge". Among those indicted are Rowland Bleed'em Dictator Morris [Robert Morris Fawcett] and Samuel Hairbrain Pead [Samuel Peed].

But, even in 19th-century Cambridge, life was not all votes and hustings. Robert Barnard issued a poster against his wife, called *The Scorpion's Caution,* in 1841, immediately followed by Martha Barnard's vengeful *Caution!!!.* An eye-catching notice inviting the populace to fireworks on the visit of Queen Victoria to Cambridge in 1843 shows the more formal side of the city. Public appeals against natural disaster were common, as witness a poster urging help for India.

Those interested in the spread of cars in English urban life will enjoy a Cambridge warning of 24 December 1862 printed by Wilson, following the passing of the Locomotives Act of 1861, that no 'locomotives might be used on the highways between nine at night and seven in the morning'. A further poster dated 19 December 1864 relaxed the prohibition, permitting three more hours in the evening and one more in the morning. A third poster, citing the Locomotives Act of 1865 and dated 10 October 1865, specifies a speed limit of two miles per hour.

The 'Spinning House' was not quite what its name suggests; it was in fact a prison-workhouse for prostitutes in Hills Road. The notice illustrated here antedates the notorious Daisy Hopkins case by several decades. On 2 December 1891, the Rev. Frederick Wallis, a pro-proctor and Fellow of Gonville & Caius College, apprehended Miss Hopkins on 2 December 1891 on a charge of 'walking with a member of the university'. Though she pleaded 'Not Guilty', Daisy Hopkins was sentenced to 14 days seclusion in Cambridge Spinning House by the Vice-Chancellor of the University, John Peile, Master's of Christ's, in accordance with the charter confirmed by Act of Parliament in 13 Eliz.ch.29. On appeal, the conviction was quashed because, in the judgment of Lord Coleridge, the charge of 'walking with a member of the university',

Fire Works.

NOTICE.

The Exhibition

OF

FIRE WORKS

WILL TAKE PLACE ON

Parker's Piece,

AT 7 O'CLOCK, ON

Wednesday

EVENING.

J. NAPIER,

Fire Works. Public notice on the occasion of the visit of Queen Victoria to Cambridge in 1843. 38 x 25½ cm. (*Cambridgehsire Collection*)

ORDER REGULATING THE USE OF LOCOMOTIVES

WITHIN THE BOROUGH OF CAMBRIDGE.

Whereas it appears to me, the Right Honourable Sir George Grey, Bart., one of Her Majesty's Principal Secretaries of State, that the use of Locomotives unless restricted, as hereinafter mentioned, on any highway within the limits of the borough of Cambridge, is dangerous and inconvenient to the public:

I hereby do, by virtue of the provisions of "The Locomotive Act, 1861," by this Order, under my hand, prohibit the use of any kind of Locomotive whatever propelled by steam or any other than animal power on the highways within the limits of the borough of Cambridge, at any time except between the hours of nine at night and seven in the morning.

Given under my hand at Whitehall, this 24th day of December, 1862.

G. GREY.

ORDER REGULATING THE USE OF LOCOMOTIVES . . . Concern for public safety against motor vehicles led to remarkable limitations in 1862. No place or printer. 34 x 21 cm. (*Cambridgeshire Collection*)

understood by the Vice-Chancellor and the defendant to imply 'for immoral purposes' (which is why she pleaded 'Not Guilty'), nevertheless did not read literally thus, as was required by law.

The Cambridgeshire Collection also offers rules and regulations of the Spinning House, and a voluminous series of 'duties of the Matron' which give a vivid picture of the kind of termagant who would have been favoured by the appointments board.

A public notice warning against the holding of lotteries, dated 1884, offers a wry comment on changing times when set against a legal lottery ticket dated 1978. The principle of lotteries is the same as it was a century ago: it is the legislators who have changed. The first legal lottery in Cambridge was drawn in August 1977.

The January and December elections of 1910 were won and lost on the questions of tariff reform and free trade, but the busy suffragettes issued handbills and posters which offered them support (often nebulous if not

Cambridge Spinning-House.

RULES AND REGULATIONS FOR THE INMATES.

Every person upon her committal shall be required to bathe and on the dress provided for her.

. She shall occupy a separate cell during her period of confine- except under peculiar circumstances, or when the house is too to allow the individual separation of all the Inmates; and in such the Vice-Chancellor or the Visiting Governor shall specify the par- ar Inmates to be confined in separate cells.

Every Inmate in separate confinement shall be provided with neans of communicating at any time with the Matron or Assistant on.

Every such Inmate shall also be provided with employment and neans of moral and religious instruction. She shall be supplied suitable books and have as much exercise in the open air as the cal Officer may deem necessary. She shall be visited frequently e Matron, Chaplain, and Medical Officer, and shall attend Divine ce and the daily Prayers, unless special directions under particular nstances should be given.

The Inmates shall keep their cells, and the furniture and uten- erein, clean and in good order. They shall be clean and neat eir persons, wash their hands and faces daily, and wash their feet the at least once a week or as often as the Matron or Medical r shall direct. They shall be allowed clean linen and clean towels st once a week.

The cells shall be locked up every night not later than 8 o'Clock; hey shall be unlocked every morning during the months of Novem- ecember, January, and February not later than 8 o'clock, and during maining months of the year not later than 7 o'clock.

The meals shall be served at such hours as the Governors from time may direct.

8. No deviation from the regular Dietary shall be made except by the authority of the Medical Officer.

9. The Inmates shall not be allowed to see their friends during the period of their confinement unless by order in writing signed by the Vice-Chancellor or some other Governor. The interview in every case between an Inmate and her friends shall be held in a room appointed for the purpose, and in the presence of the Matron or other Officer of the house, and shall be for a quarter of an hour only, except in special cases to be determined by a Governor.

10. No Inmate shall disobey the orders of the Matron or other Officer of the house; or treat with disrespect any of the Officers or servants or any person visiting the house or employed therein; or be idle or negligent in her work, or wilfully damage the same; or absent herself without leave from Divine Service or the daily Prayers, or behave irreverently thereat; or be guilty of any indecent or immoral language or conduct; or use any provoking or abusive words; or converse or hold intercourse with any other Inmate in a way not authorized by the Rules of the house; or cause annoyance or disturbance by singing, or making a noise; or pass or attempt to pass out of her cell, or beyond the bounds of the room or place where she may be employed; or disfigure the walls or other parts of the house; or deface, secrete, destroy, or pull down any paper or notice hung up by authority in or about the house; or wilfully injure any clothing, bedding, or other article; or commit any nuisance; or have in her cell or possession any article not furnished by the Establishment; or give or lend to or borrow from any other Inmate any food, book, or other article without leave; or refuse or neglect to conform to the Rules, Regulations and Orders of the House.

The Matron may examine any Inmate touching such offences, and determine thereupon; and may cause any Inmate so offending to be punished by being closely or otherwise confined in a dark or light cell, or by being fed on bread and water, or by both such punishments for any term not exceeding three days.

11. Well conducted Inmates may be selected and employed by the Matron to assist in the kitchen and stores, and in cleaning the house.

Cambridge Spinning-House. Wall-poster for each room of the Spinning-House in Cambridge. No place, printer, or date, but *c.* 1870. 35 x 43 cm. (*Cambridgeshire Collection*)

downright evasive) from the Liberal candidates S.O. Buckmaster, the Hon. E.S. Montagu and Sir Charles D. Rose, as well as from the Conservative candidate Almeric H. Paget.

On 9 February 1933, the Oxford Union passed their historic, notorious motion 'That this House will in no circumstances fight for its King and Country', but it is not generally remembered how strong was the pacifist feeling at the same time in Cambridge. As well as the handbill illustrated here, I have a rare 44-page pamphlet, *Cambridge University and War* (printed by W. Heffer, n.d. but 1935), written for the Co-ordinating Committee for Research into the Use of the University for War, which represented no fewer than five university groups, predominantly of the political Left.

Every election is a source of abundant street literature, mainly in the form of wall posters and handbills delivered by canvassers. Radio, television, and the daily newspapers undoubtedly have an impact on voters, but it is

GENERAL ELECTION.

To the Electors of Cambridge.

Mark what your PARLIAMENTARY CANDIDATES say about

WOMEN'S SUFFRAGE

In their Election Addresses.

Borough:

Mr. S. O. BUCKMASTER: "It should also be an essential feature of our policy to establish yet firmer the principle of representative government, and for this purpose to remove the anomalies and inequalities of our present electoral system. As part of such reform it is to my mind just and for the general good that **women, who now share the burdens, should also share the responsibilities of the State."**

Mr. ALMERIC PAGET: "While doubting if the majority of the women of this country yet desire such a change, **I am prepared, when the question arises, to support a Measure which will extend the Suffrage by removing the disqualification of sex."**

West Cambridgeshire:

The Hon. E. S. MONTAGU: "I hope that in the new Parliament the Liberal Government . . . will carry out **the reform of our Electoral and Franchise Systems, including . . . the Enfranchisement of Women."**

East Cambridgeshire (Newmarket Division)

Sir CHARLES D. ROSE: "I would support a measure for the Parliamentary Enfranchisement of Women."

Printed and Published by the "Cambridge Daily News," Ltd.

General Election. Pro-Suffragette han[d]bill of 1910 printed at the *Cambrid[ge] Daily News*. 22½ x 14cm. (*Autho[r's] Collection*)

"FORGOTTEN MEN"

reminds us of the horror, the world-wide suffering and destruction caused by the last war.

Now A NEW WORLD WAR is threatened. The last few days have made this apparent to all.

Surely this film must make us feel that there must be no more war, and that we must do our best to prevent another.

But the film itself draws no such conclusion. The pamphlet advertising "**Forgotten Men**" says: "No Government has struggled harder to avoid war than the present one. The only way to preserve peace under the present conditions is to be prepared."

Prepared for what? For another WAR!

At the present time the Government is spending an extra 10 million on the armed forces. Armament races don't prevent wars: they help to produce them. This film, which records the suffering of the last war, but which supports the war policy of the National Government, is being used to persuade us to prepare for another!

The National Government is preparing for war.

How is war to be prevented?

Not by increasing armaments, but by organising resistance of all sections of the people, by co-operating with the people of other countries.

The horrors of the next war will be a hundred times greater than the last.

You must help to prevent it

SUPPORT THE CAMBRIDGE ANTI-WAR COUNCIL

Join the Individual Members' Section

(Secretary, Mrs. Rhees, 65, Oxford Road, Cambridge)

(Issued on behalf of the Cambridge Anti-War Council and the Cambridge Scientists' Anti-War Group)

Foister & Jagg, St. Andrew's Hill, Cambridge

"FORGOTTEN MEN". Anti-war handb[ill] printed by Foister and Jagg *c*.1934. 22 [x] 14 cm. (*Author's Collection*)

probably door-to-door propaganda which has the greatest effect on the great majority of the electorate, and street literature is thus likely to continue to play a significant part in Cambridge politics.

Probably no similar confrontation of abuse and intolerance occurred in English political life from the Oswald Mosley 'Blackshirts' until the campaign of the National Front in the 1970s, when the vociferous extremists of the Left attempted to win popular support by attacking the new extremists of the Right, who had in any case never won popular support. It is therefore only to be expected that street literature, in the form of wall posters, and handbills distributed to each voter, would reflect the political pressures in the Cambridge of the 1970s in the pro-Front and anti-Front leaflets illustrated.

DO YOU CARE ABOUT YOUR COUNTRY?

The National Front is Britain's fastest growing political party. Its membership is comprised of people who are dedicated to putting Britain and the British people first. People from all walks of life and of all ages belong to the National Front; factory workers, clerical workers, shop workers, professional people, ex-servicemen and women, self employed tradesmen, post office workers, trades unionists, farmers and farm workers, housewives, shopkeepers and other small business people, local authority workers, retired folk and students, all working together to build a better Britain.

If you care about your country and care about its future, join the National Front. Whoever you are, wherever you are, there's a place for you in the National Front.

Some National Front policies:

- Put Britons first in housing, jobs, welfare and education.
- Stop immigration.
- Get Britain out of the Common Market.
- Renew ties with Canada, Australia, New Zealand and South Africa.
- Stop foreign take over of British North Sea oil.
- Resist communist take over of Trades Unions.

HELP BUILD A BETTER BRITAIN WITH THE NATIONAL FRONT.

The National Front. 1976. Political handbill distributed to households in Cambridge but printed outside the city. 21 x 15 cm. (*Author's Collection*)

WOULD YOU VOTE FOR

HITLER?

VOTE FOR A

DEMOCRATIC CANDIDATE

DON'T VOTE NATIONAL FRONT

Would you vote for Hitler? 1976. Political handbill printed by Bluebell in Cambridge. 19 x 11½ cm. (*Author's Collection*)

Further Reading

Barnicoat, John. *A concise history of posters*. London, 1972.

Fawcett, William Milner. 'Of parliamentary elections at Cambridge sixty years ago.' In *Procs. Cambridge Antiquarian Soc.*, vol. 9. N.S., Vol. 3, 1894-8, pp.166-72.

Gallo, Max. *The poster in history*. London, 1974. [N.B. The paperback ed. of 1975 is abridged.]

Hillier, Bevis. *Posters*. London, 1969.

Lewis, John Noel Claude. *Collecting printed ephemera*. London, 1976.

Lewis, John Noel Claude. *Printed ephemera: the changing use of type and letterforms in English and American printing*. London, 1962.

Rickards, Maurice. *The public notice: an illustrated history*. Newton Abbot, 1973.

Playbills and Show Posters

Mysteries, moralities, and miracle plays were performed in Cambridge churches and secular halls and open spaces in the early Middle Ages. Guilds and fraternities are also known to have acted plays in Cambridge around 1350. Dramatists of Cambridge during the 16th and 17th centuries include Ben Jonson and Robert Greene (St John's) and John Fletcher and Christopher Marlowe (Corpus Christi), but little in the way of posters or handbills survives before the 18th century, despite the acknowledged popularity of performances at Sturbridge Fair. Town and Gown confrontation occurred in 1701, when the Mayor permitted a company of actors to perform at the Fair. Dr. Bentley, then Vice-Chancellor, sent Doggett the actor to gaol and ordered the theatre booth to be destroyed.

The Norwich drama company expanded its annual Autumn tour late in the 18th century to visit Cambridge for three weeks, and the earliest playbill for Cambridge I have seen (illustrated here) shows a performance of Sheridan's *The Rivals* in 1791, probably at a theatre on the Newmarket Road close to the fairground. The Norwich tour continued until about 1852.

The star-system began about 1828. Visitors to the Theatre Royal Barnwell (erected in 1808 to designs by William Wilkins, architect of Downing College and the National Gallery), included Sheridan Knowles, who appeared as Virginius in the popular tragedy of that title in 1833; Macready, playing Macbeth, Othello and William Tell; Charles Kemble, Ellen Tree and Miss Foote. Charles Kean played at Cambridge in 1860.

On Horse Fair night it was customary to mount George Lillo's tragic melodrama *George Barnwell* (1730), perhaps taking advantage of the accidental identity of the hero's name with the place of performance. Set at Camberwell Grove, in London, the plot concerns an apprentice who, seduced by the arts of a vile woman (aha!), murders his uncle, but is then betrayed by his seducer and ends on the scaffold. The violence of the play was often reflected by fighting in the pit.

Amateur theatre in Cambridge, predominantly inspired by university and college groups, was organized as long ago as 1830, when the Shakespeare Club was founded; it was succeeded by the Garrick Club (1834-42) and other, short-lived societies, such as the Cambridge Amateur Theatrical Society inaugurated in 1855 to give charity performances for widows and orphans of

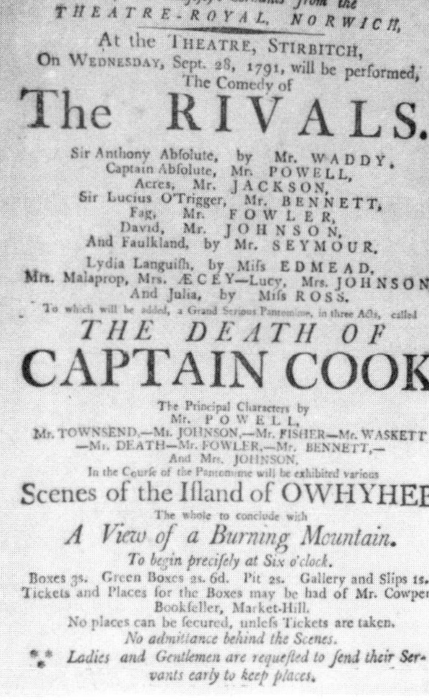

Theatre, Stirbitch. Playbill for Sheridan's *The Rivals* and the 'grand serious pantomime' *The Death of Captain Cook*, performed at Sturbridge Fair, Cambridge, 1791. 24 x 19 cm. (*Cambridgeshire Collection*)

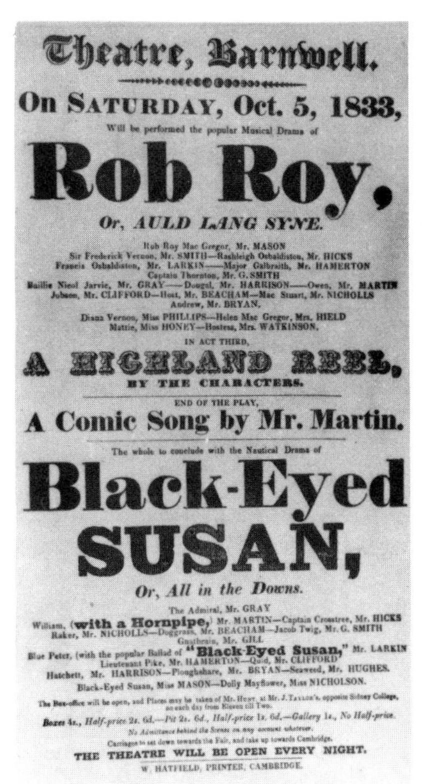

Theatre, Barnwell. Playbill for the musical *Rob Roy* and the burlesque 'nautical drama' *Black-Eyed Susan*, 1833. 26 x 14 cm. (*Cambridgeshire Collection*)

Crimean War victims. One recalls such famous societies as the Footlights (founded in 1883 and perhaps stronger in the 1960s and 1970s than ever before); the Rodney Dramatic Club (founded in 1899); the Marlowe Society (founded to perform Elizabethan plays, in 1908); the Cambridge University Mummers (founded in 1928 by Alistair Cooke; yes, *the* Alistair Cooke) and – above all – the Amateur Dramatic Club.

A.D.C. playbills can be found in Cambridge University Library guardbook Add. 7675, covering the period from the founding of the club in 1855 by F.C. Burnand, as 'Tom Pierce' both actor and manager, to the year 1911.

Most of the early playbills bore no printer's imprint, those which did emanating chiefly from the office of F.W. Talbot at 19 Sussex St. Beginning in 1867, W. Metcalfe printed them from Green Street. Spalding's of Green Street printed most of the playbills and programmes for the A.D.C. from

1878, but that for *The Day of Reckoning*, a 3-act play by J.R. Planche, was printed by F.C. Gower Litho of St. Edward's Passage. Changes occurred when a more sober format was introduced by the University Press from 1886. Then, from 1889, W.P. Spalding of 43 Sidney St resumed some of the A.D.C.'s work until the University Press again took over for the period 1893-1911, reintroducing staid typography, a demure format, and monochrome printing. The typographical history of the A.D.C. is characteristic of the other city institutions, wavering between University Press and city printers as costs, influence and personalities fluctuated over the years.

Originally exclusive, with only two rooms at the back of the Hoop Hotel in Jesus Lane, and expanding in 1860 to a new set of rooms, the A.D.C. first admitted women in 1861 and did not regularly welcome the public to performances until after World War I. The present theatre was opened in 1935.

University theatre in Cambridge was saved by regular grants from the University from 1964; in 1973, the University leased the premises and began to manage the A.D.C. as a University playhouse.

The Bijou Dramatic Club, founded by William Beales Redfern in 1875, performed first in the Victoria Assembly Rooms, on the east side of Market Square, but in 1882 Redfern bought the disused skating rink in St Andrew's St which had once been a theatre, and called it the Theatre Royal (not to be

A. D. C.

THIS EVENING WILL BE PRESENTED,

A FAST TRAIN! HIGH PRESSURE!! EXPRESS!!!

Colonel Jack Delaware . . . . Mr. G. SEYMOUR.
Griffin . . . . Mr. TOM PIERCE.
Biffin . . . . Mr. A. HERBERT.

TO BE FOLLOWED BY THE BURLESQUE TRAGIC OPERA,

BOMBASTES FURIOSO.

Artaxominous *(King of Utopia)* . . . . . Mr. TOM PIERCE.
Fusbos . . . . Mr. T. KING.
General Bombastes . . . . Mr. JAS. BEALE.
Distaffina . . . . Mr. C. DIGBY.

ARMY, COURTIERS, &c., &c.

TO CONCLUDE WITH

DID YOU EVER SEND YOUR WIFE TO CAMBERWELL?

Chesterfield Honeybun . . . . Mr. TOM PIERCE.
Crank . . . . Mr. W. SMITH.
Mrs. Honeybun . . . . Mr. C. DIGBY.
Mrs. Crank . . . . Mr. T. KING.
Mrs. Jewell . . . . Mr. R. JOHNSON.

Acting Manager—TOM PIERCE, Esq. *Stage Manager*—N. YATES, Esq.
Prompter—J. SHEPHERD, Esq.
Scenery and Appointments by S. J. E. JONES, Esq.

CAMBRIDGE GREEK PLAY COMMITTEE

THE ANTIGONE OF SOPHOCLES

will be performed IN THE ORIGINAL GREEK *by Members of the University*

with Music specially composed by P. A. TRANCHELL, M.A., Mus.B.

at the ARTS THEATRE, CAMBRIDGE

(Half-a-minute from King's Parade and the Market Square)

TUESDAY—SATURDAY, 24th—28th FEBRUARY, 1959

at 2.15 p.m. daily

Also on Wednesday at 8.0, Thursday at 5.0, Friday at 8.0, Saturday at 8.15

Producer:
ALAN KER, M.A., Trinity College

Musical Director:
P. A. TRANCHELL, M.A., Mus.B., King's College

Settings and Costumes:
M. A. S. BURGESS, Ph.D.

PRICES OF SEATS

Boxes (for five) £2 0s. 0d. (Saturday night: £2 12s. 6d.)
Stalls and Dress Circle: 8/-, 6/6, 5/-. (Saturday night: 10/6, 8/-, 6/6 and 5/-)

confused with the Barnwell theatre of the same name). There he put on the first of the plays in Classical Greek in 1882, and though he demolished it, he reopened the New Theatre on the same site in 1896. The New Theatre became Cambridge's tenth cinema in the 1930s.

The tradition of the play in Classical Greek, beginning with the *Ajax* of Sophocles, survives virtually uninterrupted to the present day, a poster here illustrating the 1959 triennial production.

The most exciting professional theatre in Cambridge's history was surely the *art nouveau* Festival Theatre in Wellington Street, built in 1926 on the site of the Theatre Royal Barnwell by Terence Gray, who thoughtfully retained the Regency auditorium of 1808 designed by Wilkins. Luckily for posterity, the Festival Theatre has been retained as a store by the Arts Theatre management. From 1926, for a glorious decade of experiment, the Festival Theatre put on the classical and modern repertory from Aeschylus to Eugene O'Neill with no regard for box-office success. Gray discovered Margaret Rawlings, Tyrone Guthrie, Flora Robson, Robert Donat, Ninette de Valois, and many more stars in the modern constellation. Style and adventure are reflected in the ambitious programmes and *Festival Review* magazines which are prized collectors' items nowadays in the field of Cambridge printed ephemera costing £1 or more each.

After the collapse of the Festival Theatre, Cambridge's need for a new theatre was met by the Keyneses, (John Maynard and his wife Lydia Lopokova), whose Arts Theatre on Peas Hill opened in 1936 with a Gala consisting of four complete ballets and the *pas de trois* from *Swan Lake*. The conductor was Constant Lambert, and among the dancers were Margot Fonteyn, Frederick Ashton, Michael Somes, and Robert Helpmann. Regrettably, the Arts Theatre collection of its own posters, programmes, and playbills is far from complete, but the current House Manager, Melvin Sullivan, is keenly aware of the value of a comprehensive archive and is steadily working towards a retrospective collection.

Sturbridge (less correctly 'Stourbridge') Fair, which belonged to the city and corporation of Cambridge, was held in September for three weeks from well before 1211 up to the present century. Sturbridge was the most important fair in all England and one of the largest in Europe, so it is well to recognize its role in the distribution of ballads and chapbooks. Tents and wooden booths were erected on open fields for the duration of the fair to form streets, and the street of 'booksellers' or stationers can be imagined as important for the staff and undergraduates of Cambridge as St. Giles' Fair was for Oxford in the 16th century.* There is no other way to account for the

* Thorold Rogers, *History of agriculture and prices in England,* vol. 1, ch. vii, p.141 for Sturbridge Fair and vol. 4, ch. iv, p.155 for St. Giles' Fair.

◁ **A.D.C.** Playbill for the opening night of the Amateur Dramatic Club, May 1855, showing the founder, F.C. Burnand, active as Tom Pierce in the roles of Acting Manager and actor. 21 x 15½ cm. (*Cambridge University Library, ADC Archives*)

◁ **CAMBRIDGE GREEK PLAY COMMITTEE.** Card poster for the traditional Classical Greek play performed in the original Greek. An appropriately plain poster printed by Severs of Cambridge, 1959. 36 x 25 cm. (*Collection of Melvin Sullivan, Arts Theatre*) rapid diffusion of books, pamphlets and street literature at a time when newspapers and advertisements were virtually unknown, and Oxford college accounts do in fact show entries for purchases of books at St. Giles' Fair.

Daniel Defoe described the great European mart in *A tour thro' the whole island of Great Britain* (vol. 1, 1724), and Sturbridge was without doubt the 'Vanity Fair' which John Bunyan reviled in *The pilgrim's progress* from first-hand knowledge.

Sturbridge Fair is not sufficiently remembered for its significant part in the distribution of books. John Dunton, in *The life and errors of John Dunton* (2 vols. in 1, 1818), says of a certain Mr Shrowsbury (a frequenter of the Fair) that he was perhaps 'the only Bookseller that understands *Fair-keeping* to any advantage'. 'Three of the booths at Stourbridge were at one time owned by a local printer, Robert Leete, who on his death in 1663 left them to his wife', according to G.J. Gray and W.M. Palmer (*Abstracts from the Wills of Printers . . . of Cambridge,* p.98). Marjorie Plant, in *The English book trade* (London, 1939; 2nd ed., 1965), quotes Lansdowne MS. 68 art. 32 to the effect that 'Sturbridge faier now drawing neere, beinge the chiefest time, wherein [a bookseller] hopeth to reape greatest fruite of this his travaile'.

Regular auctions of books, nowadays virtually confined to the great London auction-houses, were a feature of Sturbridge Fair. Among the chapmen hawking their ballads, chapbooks and almanacks there were the established booksellers and itinerant auctioneers. Edward Ward, in *A step to Stir-Bitch-Fair* (London, 1700), gives a marvellously satirical account of his visit to Sturbridge Fair: '[Garlick Row] terminates in a Place call'd originally *Cooks-Row*, but now more properly *Cuckolds-Row*, from the great Number of Booksellers that are now crept into Possession of their Greasinesses Division; this Learned part of the Fair is the Schollars chief Rendezvouz, where some that have Money come to buy Books, whilst others who want it, take 'em slily up, upon Condition to pay if they're catch'd, and think it a Pious piece of Generosity, to give St. *Austin* or St. *Gregory* Protection in a Gown Sleeve till they can better provide for 'em. Here the most famous Auctioneer of all Great as well as Little *Britain,* sells Books by the Hammer, and gives the Scholars as merry an Entertainment, as a Mountebank and his *Andrew*.

"Here's an Old Author for you, Gentlemen, you may judge his Antiquity by the Fashion of his Leather-Jacket; herein is contain'd, for the Benefit of you Scholars, the Knowledge of every thing; written by that famous Author, who thro' his Profound Wisdom, very luckily discover'd that he knew nothing! For your Encouragement, Gentlemen, I'll put him up at two Shillings, advance 3 Pence; Two Shillings one: What no Body bid?"

"The Bidder advances 3d. Two and 3d. once: Gentlemen, Fye for shame, why sure Men of your Parts and Learning, will never suffer the Works of so famous an Author to be thus undervallued: If you'll believe me, Gentlemen, he's worth more to a Powder-Monkey to make Cartridges of, than what's bid: Two and three pence twice? What no Body amongst you Gentlemen of

Strawberry Fair. Handbill using red as a second colour and printed on recycled paper in Cambridge, 1977. 29½ x 21 cm. (*Author's Collection*)

the Black Robe, that has so much respect for the Wisdom of our Ancestors, as to advance t'other 3d? Well Sir, I find you must have him at two and three pence [Knock] and now you've bought him: Sir I must tell you, you'll find Learning enough within him, to puzzle both Universities: and thus much I promise you further Sir, when you have read him seven years, if you don't like him, bring him to me again, in *Little Brittain*, and I'll help you to a Man shall give you a Shilling for him, to cover Band-Boxes". At this sort of rate he banters the young Studients; and whatever they purchas'd, gave 'em a Jest into the Bargain'.

In 1686, the celebrated London auctioneer Millington sold the library of James Chamberlain, a Fellow of St. John's. Isaac Newton, as a freshman at Trinity, bought at Sturbridge not only his famous prism but also his first book on astronomy though finding to his disgust that he could not understand it due to his ignorance of geometry and trigonometry.

A plan of Sturbridge Fair made in 1725 shows Booksellers' Row to be the first on the right entering Garlick Row from Cheapside (nowadays the Newmarket Road).

Weekend ticket £5.00
One day ticket £3.00
All day buffet and bars Camping sites available
Off site car park within 50 yards of entrance
Two indoor stages for evening performances & club tent
Tickets from Central Library Box Office Lion Yard Cambridge
Telephone (0223) 57851
Promenade Concert with James Galway on Thursday July 28
John Holder '77
The Thirteenth Cambridge Folk Festival
Weekend of July 29 30 31 1977
Cherry Hinton Hall grounds
Ralph McTell Don McLean The Boys of the Lough The David Bromberg Band Bert Jansch
The Albion Dance Band Martin Carthy Alex Campbell Bill Keith, Tony Rice & David Grisman
Vin Garbutt Cousin Joe from New Orleans Jean Redpath Bernard Wrigley Magna Carta
Johnny Silvo Andy Irvine and Paul Brady Bill Caddick Hunters' Moon Fred Wedlock
Jim Page Joanne Carlin Stephen Wade Dick Fegy The Tannerhill Weavers
Telephone Bill and The Smooth Operators Frances Gilvray and Mick Burke Mike Elliot
Saffron Summerfield Holly Tannen Brian Cookman Johnny Morris Flakey Pastry

The Thirteenth Cambridge Folk Festival. Handbill produced in Cambridge 1977. 21 x 15 cm. *(Author's Collection)*

William Chapman, in *The Bookworm* (1888), is our witness to the decline of the sale of literature in Sturbridge Fair. "Stourbridge Fair", he reports, "was the most important book fair in the kingdom, probably on account of its contiguity to Cambridge. Here came grave dons and festive students from the universities, and it must have been a very interesting sight in those days; even now, though there are no bookstalls, it is one of the noisiest fairs to be found in England".

Though Sturbridge Fair died with the spread of the car, with the increasing sophistication of shopping and due to attrition by other forms of entertainment, less ambitious fairs still flourish. Among them are Midsummer Fair (nowadays of the swings-and roundabouts variety), and Strawberry Fair (with craft stalls, rustic sports, street theatre, and alternative technology displays such as recycling machines, heat pumps, and solar heating devices). The Cambridge Folk Festival, organized by the City Council, has become a national event, with increasingly attractive posters such as the 1977 example illustrated here, by John Holder.

One may collect a variety of ballet ephemera, such as the bills issued for the Royal Ballet season under the big top on Jesus Green in 1977, and the Cambridge Ballet Workshop posters. Or college society ephemera, still a largely untilled field. Film ephemera from the Arts Cinema and filmshow groups. Opera bills from the Guildhall and the Arts Theatre. Concert bills from the Guildhall, King's College Chapel and the numerous other venues. Wrestling and pop music handbills from the Corn Exchange.

The acquisition of contemporary printed street literature in Cambridge (a prerequisite for studying it) is a hobby for those with boundless energy, time, storage space, imagination, persistence, and friends. Particularly friends.

Further Reading

Theatres

Burnand, Francis Cowley. *The 'A.D.C.'; being personal reminiscences of the University Amateur Dramatic Club.* London, 1880. [By the founding actor-manager of the A.D.C.; covers only period up to 1864]

Higgins, Norman. *The Cambridge Arts Theatre, 1936-1968: a personal record.* Cambridge, [1978]

Keynes. Florence Ada. *By-ways of Cambridge history.* 2nd ed. Cambridge, 1956. [This revised ed. is the first containing a general account of drama in Cambridge]

Mackintosh, Iain. 'The Festival Theatre, 1808 and 1926'. In *Granta*, vol. 74, no. 2, November 1968, pp.6-9.

Melling, John Kennedy. *Discovering theatre ephemera.* [Aylesbury] 1974.

Fairs

Caraccioli, G. *An historical account of Sturbridge, Bury, and the most famous fairs in Europe and America.* Cambridge, 1753.

Nichols, J. *The history and antiquities of Barnwell Abbey, and of Sturbridge Fair.* London, 1786.

COLLECTING AND STUDYING CAMBRIDGE STREET LITERATURE

No other collection can be so easily or so cheaply acquired as a collection of printed ephemera produced in one's own city: some of it is indeed pushed through one's letterbox willy-nilly. However, a collection of street literature is somewhat more discriminating, in the sense that the content must have at least a minimal literary content, as opposed to the credit cards, bus tickets, or business cards which are purely utilitarian, and carry no message more durable than that of immediate identification for a specific purpose. Yet the literary content is not that of *belles-lettres*, already served by numerous libraries collecting printed books and periodicals which would even deny the more pretentious name of 'literature' to some of the categories arbitrarily included here.

Perhaps the most enlightened collection in its deliberately all-embracing policy of inclusion is the **Cambridgeshire Collection**, Central Library, Lion Yard, Cambridge, to whose expert staff the present study owes a major obligation for text and plates alike. This collection is not only the premier source for non-university materials reflecting the life and history of the old county (Huntingdon and Peterborough Local Studies collections cover their respective areas within the new county), but it is also a model of how to run a local studies collection, since the staff neglect *no aspect*, including the most ephemeral of printed matter (such as paper bags issued by Cambridge shops) or even mimeographed notices of local society meetings.

As regards street literature, the Cambridgeshire Collection will satisfy most researchers on posters, handbills, playbills and other showbills, and is particularly strong in political notices and squibs, and city council posters.

The Cambridgeshire County Record Office, Shire Hall, Castle Hill, contains not only the usual census and directory material, but also sale and election notices, in which it is very strong. **Cambridge University Library** has a collection of university-biased ephemera that complements to a large extent the city and county-biased Cambridgeshire Collection; yet CUL is the best source for the late ballads emanating from Cambridge and the Map Room is perhaps not sufficiently well known as a source of sale and auction notices, mainly from the early 1860s.

Recently the **Cam Papers** collection in Cambridge University Library has been improved by vigorous acquisition by enthusiastic staff who are, however, overworked as a result of current financial restrictions. This source should thus be regarded as a last resort; a special admissions ticket is necessary to read in CUL.

Categories of material kept conveniently in large folders in **Cambridge and County Folk Museum** include trade catalogues and advertisements; theatre programmes and playbills; menus; lamplighter's verses (1844 and 1862); hospitals and prisons; election notices and squibs; municipal notices; schools; proctorial system; appeals; University Volunteer Rifle Corps; the Cattle Market; Crane's Charity; churches; transport.

The student of Cambridge printed street literature should be aware of a national collection which as it happens is housed in the English Faculty, Cambridge University, and is consequently limited to those with access to the English Library. Joan T. Black of the Faculty Library is also Hon. Librarian of the **Library of Contemporary Culture Records**, a registered charity founded in 1970. The LCCR is concerned with documents illustrating thought, policy and activity in areas traditionally considered 'cultural' – the fine arts, music, theatre and literature, and such related subjects as tourism, adult education, literacy and the consumer society. Only two of the trustees in 1977 resided outside Cambridge, so it is clear that the location and personalities involved favour the collection of Cambridge literature. Ephemera naturally constitute the bulk of the library, though there are periodical runs and sets of government reports, often lacking many parts since the LCCR relies on donations of material and cash for its running costs: demands from outsiders should therefore be kept to a minimum.

Almanacks

Cambridge almanacks are best consulted in Cambridge University Library, the British Library (London), and the Bodleian Library, Oxford.

Ballads and Broadsides

The only worthwhile collection of the few ballads printed in Cambridge is in the Madden Collection, Rare Books Room, CUL. The Cambridge-printed ballads are listed in the foregoing text.

Chapbooks

For various reasons there were virtually no chapbooks printed in Cambridge (see text).

Posters and Handbills

The C.H. Cooper collection of posters and similar leaflets connected with the city is to be found, with a mass of related ephemera of all periods from the 18th century onwards, in the **Cambridgeshire Collection**.

The J.W. Clark collection of predominantly university ephemera, together with other material principally of the 19th and 20th centuries, is to be found in the **Cam Papers** of the CUL.

The John Johnson Collection in the **Bodleian Library** has a wide range of all kinds of Cambridge posters and handbills.

Playbills and Show Posters

The Cambridgeshire Collection has a rich and varied selection of Cambridge playbills from the 18th century onwards, with especial strength in the 19th century. The CUL **Rare Books Room** has on loan the ADC Archives, and the courtesy of the Amateur Dramatic Club committee in permitting consultation of these archives and reproduction from them is hereby gratefully acknowledged. The **Arts Theatre**, thanks to the energy of the present House Manager, now possesses a near-complete file of its own posters. Cambridge City Council Amenities Department kindly agreed to the illustration of one of their attractive posters.

The Cambridgeshire Collection has a good collection of handbills connected with Midsummer Fair and Sturbridge Fair (1860-1915).

Collectors of Cambridge ephemera would do well to join the Ephemera Society, which publishes *The Ephemerist*; to subscribe to *Exchange and Mart* for its regular advertisements of printed ephemera; to browse in the bookshops of David in St. Edward's Passage, Galloway and Porter in Sidney St., Derek Gibbons in Green St., and Jean Pain and Deighton & Bell in Trinity St.; to watch out for postcard auctions such as those of Ken Lawson (Middlesex Collectors' Centre, 24 Watford Road, Wembley) which invariably include printed ephemera; and to attend provincial booksellers' fairs such as those held in Cambridge Corn Exchange in 1977 and the Guildhall in 1978, antiques fairs, and collectors' fairs generally. One gradually becomes known as a collector of Cambridge street literature, and one will begin to specialize.

Enterprising exhibitions are held every so often: one recalls D.J. Hall's exhibition on the Amateur Dramatic Club in 1975 showing playbills and other ephemera in Cambridge University Library; Gordon Shaw's display of street literature in the Cambridge College of Arts and Technology in 1976; and Michael Petty's show devoted to Cambridge street literature in Cambridge Central Library in 1978. Poem posters were specially printed and shown to mark the Cambridge Poetry Festival.

General Bibliography

Cambridge

Bartholomew, A.T. *Catalogue of the books and papers relating to the Town and County of Cambridge, bequeathed by J.W. Clark*. Cambridge, 1912.

Bowes, R. *A catalogue of books printed at or relating to the University, Town and County of Cambridge from 1521 to 1893.* Cambridge, 1894.

Street Literature

Bodleian Library, Oxford. *The John Johnson Collection: catalogue of an exhibition.* Oxford, 1971.

Chalmers, G.S. *Reading easy 1800-50: a study of the teaching of reading, with a list of the books which were used, and a selection of facsimile pages.* 'The Broadsheet King', 15 Mortimer Terrace, London NW5, 1976.

Collison, Robert L. *The story of street literature, forerunner of the popular press*. London, 1973.

Mayhew, Henry. *London labour and the London poor*. 4 vols. New York, 1968. [Following the original edition of 1861. Material on street literature is to be found mainly in vol. 1.]

Neuburg, Victor E. *Popular literature: a history and guide from the beginning of printing to the year 1897.* Harmondsworth,1977. [Good bibliography]

Shepard, Leslie. *The history of street literature.* Newton Abbot, 1973.